ONBOARDING
MATTERS

Praise for *Onboarding Matters*

"I've seen first-hand across many software-as-a-service (SaaS) companies how successful onboarding sets customers on a path to accelerated outcomes—and inversely how poor onboarding is a fast track to churn. *Onboarding Matters* provides an impactful framework, as well as practical tips and valuable resources, to perfect the art and science of a superior onboarding process. It's a must read for anyone who cares about Customer Success."

— Ashvin Vaidyanathan, Author of *The Customer Success Professional's Handbook: How to Thrive in One of the World's Fastest Growing Careers—While Driving Growth for Your Company*, and Chief Customer Officer, Gainsight

"One of the biggest challenges and obstacles to growth today is the ability to understand and align with customers on their desired business outcomes. It starts with onboarding. When you deliver a proactive and prescriptive experience, as defined in *Onboarding Matters*, your customers reach their goals and so do you."

— Matthew E. May, Author of *The Elegant Solution* and *Winning the Brain Game*

"*Onboarding Matters* by Donna Weber is the leading guide for anyone seeking to create a high-impact onboarding program. The book is a step-by-step blueprint for orchestrating Customer Success from day one. I always say that customer onboarding is the beginning of churn or success, and Donna's book takes you through the why and the how. A must-read with clear examples and resources to apply to your organization."

— Emilia D'Anzica, Founder, Growth Molecules

"Do yourself and your customers a favor and read *Onboarding Matters*! Customer Success leaders will benefit from Donna's conclusions on the importance of onboarding and its impact on the rest of the customer journey. The C-suite will be thrilled about the future earnings an orchestrated approach drives."

— Kristen Hayer, CEO of The Success League and Top 25 Customer Success Influencer

"*Onboarding Matters* shines a bright light on a dark corner of the subscription economy: taking care of new customers. Orchestrated Onboarding helps customers gain faster and bigger value from your product, which is critical for your subscription business."

— Brian Gentile, Board Chairman and CEO Coach

"The customer journey doesn't stop with the sale. In fact, bringing customers onboard is the most important part of the customer journey. With insight and practical knowledge, Donna reveals how to truly drive Customer Success. A must read for leadership teams."

— Mike Gospe, Customer Advisory Board Strategist, Co-founder of KickStart Alliance

"After working closely with Donna Weber, I experienced first-hand how the Orchestrated Onboarding framework is applied to fast growing companies. *Onboarding Matters* provides a practical, easy-to-follow roadmap for creating positive first impressions and impactful customer experiences."

— Rod Cherkas, Professional Services Executive at Gainsight and Marketo

"When it comes to proving value and earning the customer's trust, what starts right, stays right. So don't leave things to chance! Adopt disciplines like the Orchestrated Onboarding framework to ensure your customers' success — and your own."

— Ed Powers, Customer Experience and Customer Success consultant

"If you are involved in recurring revenue business models, you are probably aware that the onboarding phase is a make or break experience. *Onboarding Matters* hammers that home, explaining clearly from first-hand experience and research the why and how to make that critical first and lasting positive impression."

— Sue Nabeth Moore, Customer Success Evangelist and Co-founder of Success Chain

"Having worked with Donna over the years, I continue to admire her deep Customer Success and Onboarding expertise and her ability to explain concepts so impactfully. There are multiple careers worth of wisdom in this book!"

— Lauren Thibodeau, Customer Experience Advisor,
Founder of SaaSCan™

"If you agree that setting customers up for success with your product is one of the best ways to maximize customer lifetime value, then you believe onboarding might be the best way to do that. Donna Weber, the world's leading expert in customer onboarding, tells you how to do it. I suggest you listen to her."

— Bill Cushard, General Manager at ServiceRocket and
host of Helping Sells Radio

"Donna Weber dispels one of the most pernicious misconceptions about customer onboarding: that it's just a matter of technical implementation. Any B2B company with an onboarding team should take note of her enablement-centered approach to helping customers actually get value from the products they bought."

— Kate Hopkins, Founder of OneGuide

"For any company looking to delight and retain customers, *Onboarding Matters* is an essential read and should be used as a manual for what to do (and what not to do) to create the best customer experiences."

— Elizabeth Jones, Vice President of Client Success at Clearwave

"Well begun is half done! Successful customer onboarding creates a lasting impression that guarantees a productive renewal conversation later. Donna outlines six stages of the Orchestrated Onboarding framework that's a must-follow for every Customer Success leader and implementation specialist."

— Shreesha Ramdas, Senior Vice President at Medallia,
Founder of Strikedeck

"Do you launch your customers with the same care that you launch your products? If not, you need this book. Read it and transform Customer Success from a job title to a reality."

— Anne Janzer, author of *Subscription Marketing*

"Onboarding is the critical period that makes or breaks customer relationships. I had the privilege of working with Donna to implement the Orchestrated Onboarding framework and I can tell you it makes a difference. *Onboarding Matters* captures everything you need to create customers for life at your company."

— Karl Van den Bergh, Chief Marketing Officer at Gigamon

"*Onboarding Matters* needs to be required reading for everyone concerned about customer retention. Donna clearly reveals the challenges that surface during customer onboarding, and provides an effective methodology to keep your customers on a sustainable course. From the very first chapter you learn what's at stake and how to have impact."

— Mikael Blaisdell, Executive Director of
The Customer Success Association

"Read this book if you want to ensure a smooth and successful launch with your customers. *Onboarding Matters* provides a practical roadmap that guarantees quick value for your customers and recurring revenue for you."

— Irene Lefton, Customer Success Executive, Advisor, Author,
and Top 25 Customer Success Influencer

"Everyone who touches a customer in a B2B organization should read this book. Not only does Donna explain why onboarding is so important, she shows you how to do this successfully. Now there's no excuse not to do onboarding right!"

— Linda Popky, President of Leverage2Market Associates and
author of *Marketing Above the Noise: Achieve Strategic Advantage
with Marketing that Matters.*

"Onboarding Matters delivers the most practical and straightforward Customer Success tutorial I have ever read. Donna does a masterful job of articulating why you can't rely on hope as a strategy. Instead it's time to bring together sales, marketing, and customer facing teams to collaborate across the buyer and customer journeys. This book will quickly become THE customer onboarding blueprint to success!"
#HopeIsNotAStrategy

— Roderick Jefferson, Vice President, Field Enablement, Author of *Sales Enablement 3.0: The Blueprint to Sales Enablement Excellence*

ONBOARDING
MATTERS

How Successful Companies
Transform New Customers
Into Loyal Champions

Donna Weber

Springboard Press

This book is dedicated to the customer.
Because when customers win, we win.

In loving memory of Dorothy Weber.

Contents

Orchestrate
Organizing and planning something that is complicated
to achieve a desired or maximum effect

Onboarding
The action or process of familiarizing new customers
with your products and services

Foreword

As I write this, we are facing an unprecedented pandemic that ranks high on the pain scale. An invisible virus, COVID-19, has brought the entire world to a screeching halt. The losses, both human and economic, are staggering. Worldwide, we have lost over 2.2M people. In the U.S. alone, COVID-19 has claimed more than 500,000 precious lives. Economically, most countries are in a recession. According to the International Monetary Fund, the global economy shrunk by 4.4 percent in 2020—the worst since the Depression of the 1930s. The road to recovery will require a concerted global effort. In other words, it will take time.

To weather the long storm, many businesses have sustained budget freezes and workforce reductions. Every corporate dollar counts now more than ever. As the pandemic remains center stage with new virus variants casting doubt on our ability to return to "normal," businesses are finally paying attention to their most valuable asset: *their* customers. Not because they suddenly care more about them (let's be honest), but because they do care about retaining their dollars and keeping the lights on. This has shined a spotlight on post-sales customer operations, otherwise known as Customer Success.

It's about time.

In a subscription business, the sale doesn't end when the deal is won. Post-sales teams have learned this the hard way. Tragically, even when the proverbial writing is on the wall, clear warning signs of customer churn or dissatisfaction often fall on deaf ears. Now that COVID-19 has brought so many businesses to their knees, more leaders and company boards are willing to listen. This is promising.

Since you're reading this book, you're already thinking about your customers. I implore you to go one step further and rethink the power dynamics at play: *You need your customers more than they need you.* Your success and growth are directly intertwined with theirs. And verbal affirmation is no longer sufficient; change is the currency and love language our customers expect at this very moment. By adopting the wisdom in this book, we can start delivering experiences that are designed not simply to retain our most valuable assets, but to help them win. As SaaS investors, executives, and business professionals, we have the power to collectively raise the standard by which we measure our own success. When our customers win, we win. It's that simple.

But how do we win together? Customer Success experts like Donna Weber have been on a conscious quest to answer this question to help companies avoid the exponential costs of failure. Churn not only burns our hard-won customer relationships and dollars, but it also torches precious bridges with internal teams and external partners. As tensions mount and emotional reserves run out, employees start packing their bags in search for the next opportunity. And so the painful cycle repeats. This is the oft-told story at many behind-the-curtain customer success confessions.

To break the cycle, we need to learn from churn and rewind the scene back to the very beginning when we first closed the deal and onboarded that new customer. Our go-to-market teams need to internalize why churn matters. More importantly, they need to know when, where, and how to play on Day Zero when Sales sounds the gong.

Lamentably, *entirely avoidable* customer onboarding challenges create unnecessary obstacles to predictable growth at SaaS companies of all sizes. Sales reps regularly throw new customers over the fence without a sufficient handoff. They frequently set unrealistic or undocumented expectations with customers that result in failures out of the gate. Implementations are often prematurely scoped or not scoped at all, creating team and customer friction. When we fail to show up with a plan, customers tragically end up onboarding themselves, stalling on payments, or asking for a refund. Executives end up spending precious time firefighting and little time actually building and scaling their companies. As one fire settles, another quickly emerges, resulting in a reactive, all-hands-on-deck appeasement of customers, and a bulge of impractical custom development requests.

The result? Lots of *preventable* downsell and churn.

As a current Customer Success advisor for software startups and scaleups, I observe that one in three retention-challenged software companies does not have a formalized customer onboarding process. What makes matters worse is that many reputable CEOs don't even realize they need one. Yet, they somehow expect their customers to magically grow their spend and renew. This is ludicrous and one of the main reasons why Customer Success leaders burn out so quickly. You can only swim against the current for so long.

Churn stings. But what stings more is knowing you could have *easily* done something about it. Naivete is a costly Achilles heel. As Donna outlines in this essential book, a whole body of neuroscience research helps explain why the first few days, weeks, and months of a customer's journey either set them (and you!) up for success or for failure. To win together, we need to adopt a *radically empathetic approach* that recenters the experience around the customer.

Rather than wait for several more churn events to get your house in order, I encourage you to start reading. Donna's Orchestrated Onboarding™ framework will give you the confidence, conviction, and compass needed to help your teams drastically reduce churn, improve employee satisfaction and productivity, and turn your customers into loyal champions. Financially, this translates into compounded growth and a higher company valuation.

If you're serious about growth, then it's time to get serious about how you onboard your customers. Onboarding matters.

— Samma Hafeez, Senior Director,
Sales and Customer Success Center of Excellence.
Insight Partners

Introduction

We were pouring expensive champagne down a bathtub without a stopper and didn't even know it. While we popped champagne bottles to acknowledge our success and teams cheered to celebrate new logos, our existing customers quietly slipped out the back door.

I didn't realize it at the time, when I was working at a company I'll call Ace Analytics. We devoted an incredible amount of time, money, and focus into attracting new customers and signing deals. While leaders fixated on reports showing how bookings kept growing, teams failed to take care of the customers we already had. We had a blind spot when it came to engaging existing customers in a meaningful way.

This story isn't unique.

Customer onboarding is a mess

Too many companies ignore their customers. I want to change that. Even though Customer Success is an established function, companies continue to miss the target during the crucial beginning of the customer relationship. Even as companies declare they are "customer-centric," as Ace Analytics did, they invest exponentially more in sales and marketing efforts than in customer retention. They don't attend to new customers, who are left to figure things out for themselves. These customers finally give up and go elsewhere. In fact, most customer churn happens during the crucial onboarding period.

The reality is that customer-facing teams are siloed. Either no one owns the process of bringing customers onboard, or it's the onerous job of one person. There's a tendency to wait until customers have problems before anyone gets involved. Rather than deploying expertise and guidance up front, customer-facing teams wait for customers to tell them what they want and need. On top of that, Customer Success teams are unable to scale. Even as Customer Success hits its stride, these teams tend to be riveted on inwardly facing issues, missing the opportunity to direct their attention on the customer.

The Orchestrated Onboarding™ framework

This book shows you how to fix customer onboarding. In these pages, you'll find a proven framework to move away from ad hoc and reactive onboarding to delivering a prescriptive journey of best practices. I developed the **Orchestrated Onboarding framework** over the course of several years, working with companies from across the world. While their products and industries are disparate, their problems remain the same. Whether providing big data or open-source solutions, manufacturing or accounting software, compliance, supply chain management, content management, learning management, customer management, or Customer Success systems—there is a constant need to engage and enable customers.

I've been passionate about engaging and enabling customers long before Customer Success hit the scene. From years of working at software startups, I can attest to the impact customer engagement has on the business bottom line. In the following pages, you'll see why the beginning of the customer relationship is the most important part of the customer journey, and you'll find a framework to truly partner with your customers from day one, and even before they become customers. I conceived of this framework while striving to improve customer retention at Ace Analytics. The Orchestrated Onboarding framework incorporates best practices from Sales, Customer Success, Customer Education, and Professional Services, and I built, tested, and refined it while working with a myriad of companies through my consulting firm, Springboard Solutions.

The concepts covered in this book consistently help high-growth companies put impactful processes in place. These practices reduce the time it takes to onboard customers and to implement products by anywhere from 20 to 80 percent. Using the Orchestrated Onboarding framework, my clients have experienced increases in customer retention ranging from 20 to 150 percent. Their customers are delighted to obtain value in the products they purchase and use. And internal teams are more motivated, less stressed, and more collaborative.

The findings in this book are also backed by extensive research. In 2020, I published the *Customer Onboarding Report*[1] the result of surveying 157 companies about their customer onboarding programs. I also interviewed several of the respondents to follow up from the survey and share their challenges and opportunities throughout this book.

Who should read this book

Whether you are a seasoned Customer Success leader or a first time Customer Success Manager, this book is for you. This book is for all customer-facing teams, including Customer Success, Customer Education, Professional Services, and Support. While the emphasis of this book is on high-growth technology companies, the Orchestrated Onboarding framework can be applied to most companies and industries and works for onboarding partners and channels as well— wherever you need to drive value quickly.

This book is worth your time if you answer **Yes** to one or more of the following questions:

- Does your business experience insurmountable churn?

- Is your company struggling to scale existing Customer Success approaches and teams?

- Is every new customer a "special snowflake" that needs to be handled with special treatment?

- Are you and your teams flying by the seat of your pants to deal with each new challenge that arises?

- Do you lack ways to consistently engage new people who use your product?

- Do you need to decrease the time it takes for customers to reach value in your product?

- Do you need to increase the total lifetime value of existing customers?

- Do you want to land and expand new accounts?

- Do you want a scalable proven framework to create customers for life?

In Part One, you'll learn why you should care about customer onboarding. Part Two details each of the six stages of the Orchestrated Onboarding framework to guide customers through the initial onboarding and beyond: **Embark, Handoff, Kickoff, Adopt, Review,** and **Expand**. Part Three aids you in using the principles of Orchestrated Onboarding to transform your company. To support you in putting the Orchestrated Onboarding framework into practice at your company, examples, resources, and templates are provided throughout the book and are also available on my website, **OrchestratedOnboarding.com**.

At the time we published *Onboarding Matters*, the world was engulfed in the COVID-19 pandemic. As a result, most companies are currently working remotely with their customers. The Orchestrated Onboarding framework works just as effective remotely or in person. In fact, as of this writing, I am working remotely with several companies across the globe to optimize their onboarding programs.

Customer Success terminology

Customer Success has its own terminology, and different organizations use different subsets of these terms. So, to get us all on the same page, here are a few definitions that are used throughout this book. (See the Glossary for more.)

Churn: A regular, quantifiable process or rate of change that occurs in a business over a period of time as existing customers are lost and new customers are added.

Cost of Customer Retention (CORE): The cost to retain existing customers

Customer Acquisition Cost (CAC): The cost associated in convincing a customer to buy a product/service

Customer Success Manager (CSM): This term is used generically throughout this book to denote the person responsible for helping customers maximize value in their products as strategic account managers

Low-touch: Providing one-to-many relationships with customers where services are delivered at scale

High-touch: Providing a very close relationship with customers, generally at a one-to-one level when assisting them with implementations and solving customer problems

Installed base: The measure of the number of units that have been sold and are being used; in software as a service for businesses, the installed base includes all the existing accounts

Recurring revenue: Revenue compounds month over month, or year over year, leading to huge profits when customers keep renewing

Renewal: Granting or obtaining an extension of the subscription

Services: Software companies generally include technical consultants to customize and implement their software solutions

Subscription: An arrangement for providing, receiving, or making use of something of a continuing or periodic nature, especially on a prepayment plan

Tech-touch: Automating services with customers so individuals at your company are not directly involved with customer interactions

Now that you understand the terminology, ready to start guiding new and existing customers to success? Read on.

PART 1

The Need for Orchestration

CHAPTER 1

Onboarding Is the Most Important Part of the Customer Journey

Closing new customers is cause for celebration. As long as you keep closing deals, your company is winning, right? Not necessarily.

Unfortunately, most companies are overly focused on getting new customers. Tara Nicholle Nelson, author of *The Transformational Consumer*, says it well, "Most companies are very focused on getting new customers into their funnel. It's a foolhardy thing and it's unsustainable as a business model to spend so much money generating new, disengaged customers. Until your company masters keeping customers engaged, it's like pouring champagne down the bathtub without a stopper."[2]

Customer Success is a growing, dynamic, and exciting field. There's hard work, a buzz in the air, a collegiate atmosphere, and a fast pace. It's like working in a hot startup company with a mission to change the world. However, many so-called customer-centric companies have a glaring blind spot: the customer. Rather than being fanatic about engaging new customers, Customer Success teams fixate on churn analysis and customer health scores. They agonize over how many accounts to assign to each Customer Success Manager, and how to design compensation for customer-facing teams. While these are all important, too much energy is focused inward—at the cost of ignoring customers.

Onboarding is the most important part of the customer journey

Bringing customers onboard is the most important part of the customer journey. Yet, despite this being so critical, poor onboarding is the main cause of churn. It's estimated that more than half of customer churn is related to poor onboarding and poor customer service.[3] See Figure 1 below. In the United States alone, avoidable customer churn is costing businesses over $136 billion a year.[4] While it's easy to blame this on poor products, the main reason customers leave your company in the first year is because they never got value from your product in the first place. They fail to launch.[5]

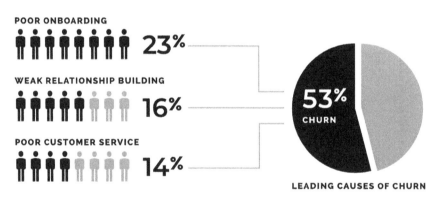

POOR ONBOARDING
23%

WEAK RELATIONSHIP BUILDING
16%

POOR CUSTOMER SERVICE
14%

53%
CHURN

LEADING CAUSES OF CHURN

Figure 1: Onboarding is the biggest cause of churn.

Most software companies have about 90 days to turn a new customer into a loyal user. Of course, the time it takes to onboard new customers might differ depending on your product. Consumer products may have only about 90 minutes to engage people, while mobile apps take 90 seconds to make a loyal user. Regardless of the category, those first days are precious because customers are most excited to be successful with your product at the very beginning.

Why customer onboarding is so important

Let's explore why the initial part of the customer journey is so critical. Resistance from new customers when you most expect them to be interested and engaged may be due to the inner workings of the brain. Customer Success expert Ed Powers, enlightened me on the neuroscience of customer interactions and how a good or bad onboarding experience could impact a customer relationship forever.

Bringing customers onboard is the most important part of the customer journey.

Neuroscience is the study of the structure and function of the nervous system and brain. Neuroscientists focus on the brain and its impact on behavior and cognitive functions, or how people think. What does neuroscience have to do with onboarding? A lot, actually. During onboarding, brain science comes into play in three areas: first impressions, buyer's remorse, and cognitive closure. While I'm no neuroscientist, I'm excited to share with you the impact onboarding has on long-term customer relationships.[6]

First impressions matter

As Ed Powers noted, not all customer interactions have equal importance. The beginning of a customer relationship directly affects the final outcome, which means the way you start with a new account may determine whether they renew or churn.[7] Those first 90 days are that important. Neuroscience offers intriguing insights into why starting on the right foot is critical for reducing churn and for building customer loyalty.

...not all customer interactions have equal importance. The beginning of a customer relationship directly affects the final outcome...

That new account you just signed is actually an organization made up of individual people. Even though the people you interact with might appear to be rational and logical, the parts of their brains activated during onboarding are those that deal with fear and value. As a result, people don't perceive the beginning of relationships objectively. Faced with uncertainty, the brain sets the first and most impactful cognitive anchor upon which all subsequent learning is based.[8] Neurobiology predisposes people to automatically place more importance on first impressions.

Confirmation bias

Split-second first judgments are so influential because subsequent information and learning reinforces the initial experience. In time, cumulative perceptions evolve into long term biases. The tendency to interpret new information as evidence of one's existing beliefs or theories is called **confirmation bias**. We embrace information that confirms our initial view while ignoring or rejecting anything that casts doubt.[9]

When your new customer has a favorable first interaction with you and your teams, they look for evidence to confirm the supportive relationship moving forward. However, when that first interaction is adverse or nonexistent, customers continually confirm their negative prejudice. They stop gathering information and stay stuck in their initial bias. It feels better to keep confirming what we already think, rather than looking for evidence that counteracts our beliefs.[10] Once the mind learns, the underlying neural patterns are difficult to change, which is why perceptions linger and opinions survive and spread. When you mess up the initial connection with new customers, you'll play catch up for a long time to come.

Buyer's remorse

Consider the personal risk buyers make when they select your product over all the choices they have: Their decision could put their reputation on the line. **Buyer's remorse** is the sense of regret after having made a purchase. It is frequently associated with large and extravagant purchases, like cars, vacations, and home purchases. However, people experience buyer's remorse even when purchasing something as insignificant as an ice cream cone. Some 82 percent of people report feeling regret or guilt over a purchase — $10 billion worth of goods, collectively.[11]

Buyer's remorse is common because of a mental process called **prospection**. Prospection means you do your best to imagine how you will think or feel in the future as a result of your decision. Your brain goes into prospection when you anticipate that fantastic vacation coming up. Your customers go into prospection during the sales process when the sales rep shares all the sensational things your product can do for them.

It seems the more involved you are with a purchase, the more intense your potential regret may be. In onboarding new customers, remember that even when the customer signs the contract, their brain keeps anticipating—conjuring up scenarios about what happens after a decision to confirm their expectations and fears. This goes on indefinitely until there's a reason to stop. That's why your onboarding program has to address the fear, remorse, and regret your buyers might have.

Cognitive closure

Since new customers' brains ruminate in fear and doubt, it's pivotal to engage them immediately. Providing a clear ending of the buyer journey and a clear beginning of the customer journey keeps customers from dwelling in buyer's remorse. When important activities do not have distinct endings, the brain keeps churning. That's where **cognitive closure** comes in. Cognitive closure is the stopping mechanism that applies "brakes" to the validating process and allows crystallized judgments to form.[12] Cognitive closure is necessary to provide a

Providing a clear ending of the buyer journey and a clear beginning of the customer journey keeps customers from dwelling in buyer's remorse.

definite answer to the questions the brain keeps asking itself. It's a way to stop the uncertainty, confusion, and ambiguity of prospection. A prescriptive onboarding process like Orchestrated Onboarding provides ways to satisfy your customer's neural networks with clear beginnings, handoffs, kickoffs, milestones, and deliverables. When customers know what's happening next, they relax and start to trust you.

The need to build trust

Consider how the people on the customer side feel. During onboarding, you move new users from what's familiar to the unknown. The buyer might feel insecure about the choice they just made and the impact it has on their organization as well as on their career. Both the project team and end users might resist having to learn to use a new tool on top of all their projects. When you leave new customers hanging without addressing all this change, they feel abandoned.

Rather than letting customers and their users ruminate, determine what you want them to think and feel after they purchase your product. Most likely, you want them to trust they're in capable hands. You want them to feel confident they made the right decision and to be excited about what's coming next. Your onboarding program needs to build confidence quickly, says Ed Powers. "The choice to churn or to renew is determined during onboarding."[13] Since customers quickly judge the value of your product and the quality of your relationship in the early days, onboarding customers in an orchestrated way is the key to helping your customers' brains engage immediately. Later in this book you'll learn ways to address those neural storms going off in their brains.

> *The choice to churn or to renew is determined during onboarding.*

Before we go further, let's take a moment to define a few terms used regularly throughout this book.

Buyer journey: The buyer journey is the sum of experiences that buyers go through when interacting with your company. Buyers interact with sales teams as they move from leads to prospects through your sales funnel.

Customer journey: The customer journey is the sum of experiences that customers go through after they sign a contract with your company. The customer journey happens after the buyer journey and customers interact with post-sales teams like Customer Success, Consulting, and Support.

Customer Onboarding: Onboarding is the action or process of familiarizing new customers with your products and your services. Customer onboarding is the first part of the customer journey and includes the following important elements: building customer relationships, implementing and going live with your product, user adoption, and change management.

In the next chapter, we'll look at the critical location of Customer Onboarding at the intersection of the buyer journey and the customer journey.

WHAT MATTERS

» Despite being so critical, poor onboarding is the main cause of churn.

» Neuroscience offers insights into customer onboarding due to first impressions, confirmation bias, buyer's remorse, and the need for cognitive closure.

» Most software companies have 90 days to turn a new customer into a loyal user. In other industries, this might be just minutes or seconds.

READY TO ONBOARD?

» List the ways your company pours champagne down the bathtub without a stopper.

» Do you know the reasons why your customers churn in their first year? In the first 30 or 90 days?

» Do you meet resistance while onboarding and enabling new customers?

» What kind of first impressions do you make with your customers?

» How long does it take to onboard new customers at your company?

CHAPTER 2

Hope is Not a Strategy for Onboarding Customers

When my friend and colleague Roderick Jefferson, a nationally recognized Sales Enablement expert, shared his tag line "Hope is not a strategy," it hit home.

Roderick validated trends I see in Customer Success all the time. Subscription software companies generally use sophisticated sales and marketing strategies to move prospects through the sales funnel, but too often they use hope as a strategy when it comes to their customers. Companies carefully align the Sales and Marketing teams, demonstrate the impact of marketing campaigns through every stage of the sales funnel, and then celebrate winning new logos. Yet, a defined post-sales customer journey is often missing.

The Customer Success Bow Tie

Despite the opportunity to grow through existing customers, companies struggle when it comes to investing in relationships with the customers they already have. Take a look at the Customer Success Bow Tie, shown below in Figure 2, which connects the buyer journey with the customer journey.

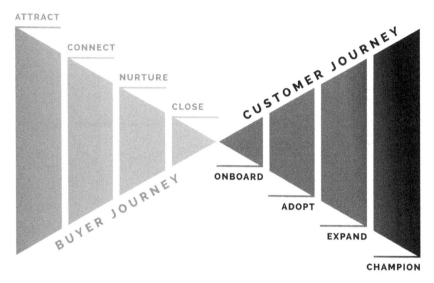

Figure 2: The Customer Success Bowtie

The buyer journey

On the left of the bowtie is the buyer journey, or sales cycle. It starts with attracting multitudes of potential buyers, narrows to nurturing qualified leads, and closes with a handful of buyers. While the sales and marketing funnel used to be ad hoc and reactive, it has matured dramatically over the last ten years. You may remember the days when Marketing and Sales teams were at each other's throats because they couldn't, or wouldn't, align. Well, that happens less frequently now with tools like Marketo, Hubspot, and Salesforce. It's common for pre-sales teams to work together on a data-driven and prescriptive buyer journey. Companies deliver digital content and online experiences to the right audience at the right time, and then measure every touch point along the digital journey. They hire sales reps who know how to interact with people and build trusting relationships. Companies use sophisticated approaches to turn leads into prospects and prospects into customers.

The customer journey

Compare the buyer experience to the customer experience after they purchase your software. The customer journey appears on the right side of the Customer Success Bow Tie. The Bow Tie shows an expansion to the right because when customers are effectively onboarded, they adopt your product, they renew, they buy more, and they become your champions. That leads to your revenue compounding and expanding. Take a look at the section between the two sides of the Bow Tie. Notice the gap between the buyer journey and the customer journey. That's because even though Customer Success is a common practice at many companies, customers are not onboarded and engaged in a meaningful way, and they fall into the gap. When you want to build long-term successful customers, you aren't just closing sales. You are opening important relationships.

Introducing Ace Analytics

Let's go back to Ace Analytics, the B2B software company I mentioned earlier. A start-up based in San Francisco, California, Ace Analytics specialized in embedded business intelligence solutions. I use Ace as a case study throughout this book, because the challenges we faced with customer onboarding, enablement, and retention are commonplace. The same gaps and issues are experienced by Customer Success teams everywhere. Similar to many companies with whom I work, the Ace Analytics product required long and complex implementations and integrations.

When I joined Ace to build the customer enablement function from scratch, I noticed the focus seemed to always be on acquiring new accounts. Sales reps rang the bell to celebrate new logos, but each signed renewal went unheeded. Leaders invested in sales and marketing resources, programs, and technology, while customer-facing teams were left in the shadows, and no one owned the customer experience. I expressed concerns that hope was our strategy when it came to engaging existing customers and suggested we build a way to create customers for life. Seizing the opportunity to build a compelling Customer Success approach at Ace, I learned from the experts, listened to customers, and brought customer-facing teams together. We built a proactive customer-facing program to move our customers and our company forward, especially during the crucial beginning of the customer relationship. That first program was the seed of the Orchestrated Onboarding framework. I saw first-hand the impact orchestrated efforts have on internal teams and customers. Throughout this book, I share the challenges we faced at Ace, how we addressed them, and the impact orchestration had.

What Ace Analytics experienced is not unique. It's a common scenario across Customer Success teams and "customer-centric" organizations. Ace had great customer programs and services: excellent customer education offerings (which I launched), highly technical professional services consultants, sharp and responsive support agents, and caring and technical customer relationship managers. However, without a clear hand-off from sales, a way to establish trusting relationships with new customers, or a defined account owner, hope was our strategy when it came to onboarding customers. We hoped customers would find their way to our services and reach success, although we never defined what success meant. When there were issues, we hoped someone internally would jump in and own the account. Ultimately, we hoped customers would renew when we contacted them 90 days before the subscription renewal.

Are you stuck in reactive heroics?

At Ace Analytics, we celebrated new logos, while customer-facing teams put out fires. We waited until new accounts struggled before we parachuted in troops to save them. We dragged busy executives into customer meetings to turn things around. We cheered heroic efforts, while the vast majority of customers were not onboarded in a meaningful way. Does this sound familiar to the Customer Success practices at your company?

Even as Customer Success gains momentum, it seems most companies still don't have formal onboarding approaches. Many companies have processes to familiarize new customers with their products and services; over 90 percent of respondents in the *2020*

Customer Onboarding Report do. The bad news is that onboarding is often ad hoc and reactive, as shown in Figures 3 and 4. Even as Customer Success gains momentum, it seems most companies still don't have formal onboarding.

New Customer Onboarding

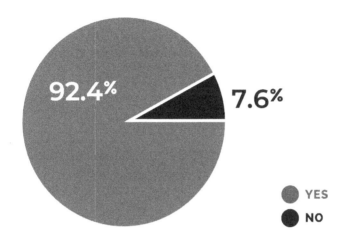

Figure 3: The 2020 Customer Onboarding Report - Do you have a process to familiarize new customers with your products and services?

Customer Journey

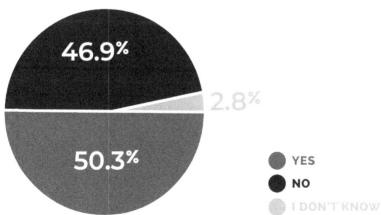

Figure 4: The 2020 Customer Onboarding Report - Have you formally mapped and documented the journey customers take after they purchase your product?

Relying on hope and heroics left Ace Analytics vulnerable to both customer churn as well as employee churn. Charging in to save customers felt good for a time, due to adrenaline rushes and high fives from colleagues and executives, but exhaustion eventually set in. The experts across the company were drained, morale dropped, and burned-out professionals headed off to less reactive companies. Waiting for customers to have problems wore out the Ace Analytics teams and put the company at risk.

Consider the overhead of saving accounts at all costs. The assumption is when you fix problem customers, those customers will stick around. Customer Success expert Greg Daines, proposes that these reactive heroics rarely work. His data from thousands of companies shows that in reality saved accounts are 50 percent less likely to renew than customers who never needed rescuing in the first place.[14]

The same was true for us at Ace Analytics. When I added up the cost of the extra hours expensive technical experts spent on reactive heroics, it came to double or triple times the license value for every account we tried to save. When you include the cost of employee turnover, this approach is too hazardous for you and for your customers.

Acquiring new customers is expensive. Really expensive.

Even though you rejoice for every new customer you sign, those same customers might depart before you can make a profit. That's because in a subscription economy, converting prospects into customers does not mean you are rolling in profits immediately. This book shows you that it's not just about getting new customers. It's about keeping the ones you already have.

The challenges are due to **customer acquisition costs** (CAC)—the cost a business incurs to acquire a new customer. CAC includes the fully loaded costs associated with sales and marketing to attract a potential customer and to convince them to purchase.[15] When you add up your expenses in sales and marketing, include employee salaries and marketing campaigns, top it with sales commissions and even prospect perks like fancy dinners, you get CAC.

Author, serial entrepreneur, and digital marketing expert Neil Patel describes CAC as the one metric that can determine your company's fate.[16] This is because acquiring new customers is expensive—really expensive. In fact, it costs up to nine times more to acquire a new customer than to keep an existing one. Figure 5 below, illustrates the time it takes to break even after acquiring new customers. (LTV in this image stands for lifetime value, which we'll cover in Chapter Eleven.) The significance of CAC is that it takes one, two, or even three renewals to make a profit on that new logo your company worked so hard to create. So, when you sign a customer and they churn in the first year, everyone loses.

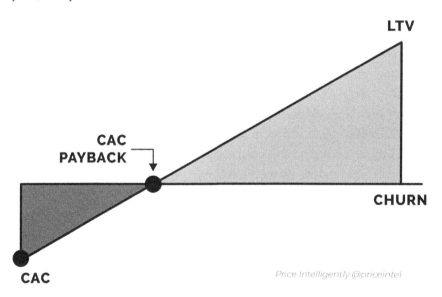

Figure 5: Customer acquisition costs and the lag time to create a profit.

When I was at Ace, we calculated it cost $1.90 for every new dollar we received to acquire new customers. That meant we lost 90 cents on each dollar during the first year of an account's life with the company. Once an account renewed, however, our investment to keep that relationship going was about nine cents on the dollar. That equates to

91 cents profit on each dollar of revenue. So, in order to make money, Ace's survival depended on new customers making it through the first year and then renewing for at least one more year, ideally for several years. The CAC image above shows that even though there's a delay in reaching that initial profit, those gains keep growing as long as existing customers keep renewing. Renewals compound over time and lead to large profits. This potential for ever increasing earnings is the reason so many companies and industries are converting to the subscription model if they haven't already.

Businesses are discovering the serious upside in the recurring revenue model, because satisfied customers are likely to keep paying for subscriptions. Take a moment to count how many software tools to which you subscribe for running your business. For my business, I use software-as-a-service (SaaS) vendors for online meetings, project management, note taking, calendaring, and bookkeeping software. Next, consider the number of subscriptions in your household. I use streaming entertainment services like Netflix and Amazon Prime, subscribe to online magazines, and listen to streaming music through Spotify and Apple Music. I also subscribe to online workout videos from Daily Burn, Les Mills OnDemand, and The Yoga Collective, and I even buy supplements and cosmetics on a subscription basis.

When companies have a strong installed base, there's an opportunity to introduce new products and services to their existing customers. Since the cost to renew and expand existing customers is a fraction of the cost for acquiring new business, this is a lucrative approach. McKinsey finds existing customers account for between a third to half of total revenue growth, even at start-ups.[17] Some companies even find their customer installed base brings in up to 80 percent of their revenue. I like to say that the longer you're around as a subscription business, the more of your revenues shift to recurring revenues from your installed base—if you're doing it correctly. Figure 6 highlights how the bulk of revenue comes from existing customers while new revenue is like the icing on the top of the cake.[18] Of course, it takes time to build to this state, which is why you need to nurture existing customers right from the start. Otherwise, you will never keep all those customers paying you year after year. The investment pays off, though, because as little as a five percent increase in customer retention produces more than a twenty-five percent increase in profits.[19]

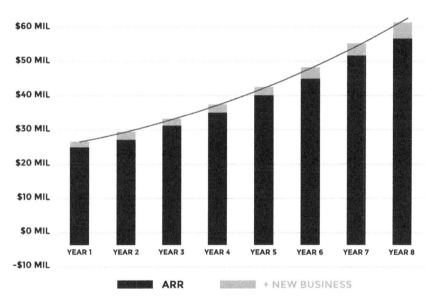

Figure 6: Installed base growth of profits

Selling to new customers without engaging them leaves your business at risk, because the costs to acquire customers eat into profits. If your teams focus on new bookings to the detriment of renewals, if you hope customers adopt your product quickly but don't show them how—don't despair. Read on to learn why engaging new customers is so important.

...the bulk of revenue comes from existing customers while new revenue is like the icing on the top of the cake.

Front-loading customer relationships

Front loading the relationship with new customers is the gateway to your success. Here are two examples.

When I interviewed the customers at a learning technology company, I was told how nice the CSMs were. When it came to onboarding, however, huge gaps were revealed. Customers told me that during kickoff meetings CSMs directed them to, "Call me when you have a problem." Those customers told me they don't want problems. They want guidance to follow the right path in the first place, instead of getting lost and having to seek help. When I shared this feedback with the company's CSMs, they were surprised to hear that customers wanted up-front direction. Working together, we built a proactive onboarding approach that guided customers through milestones and deliverables during those critical first 90 days. As a result, this company aligned Customer Success and Sales teams, guided customers along a proactive journey, and reduced their new customer onboarding time by 80 percent.

I worked with a startup that provides tools to develop web-based applications. They had just launched their first Customer Success team of three CSMs. Unfortunately, since their main responsibility was customer renewals, these individuals focused on the last 90 days while customers kept churning. They were so swamped chasing down accounts to renew, they never had a chance to engage new customers. Working with the new head of Customer Success, we dug into the churn data and learned the majority of accounts left in the first 30 days. With this important evidence in hand, we convinced the leadership team to shift CSM focus away from license renewal to onboarding and enabling customers immediately. They moved from a reactive and expensive approach to engaging customers where and when the data showed it was most needed

From touchpoint to journeys

When I was at Ace, we realized reactive heroics no longer worked. I brought cross-functional teams together to build a cohesive strategy.

We started by breaking down silos and included CSMs, course developers, implementation consultants, support agents, and the customer marketing team to map the customer onboarding journey and beyond. We documented a clear process to guide customers to milestones and deliverables along their way to success, regardless of the team with which customers engaged.

Unfortunately, I don't often observe the kind of collaboration we had at Ace Analytics. I see teams so busy reactively managing accounts, producing content, closing tickets, and delivering training and consulting that they don't see the larger customer journey. When I spoke with a company that provides software for sports teams and group activities, I learned that while they have an onboarding team, they fail to connect with other teams to build long-term customer relationships. The onboarding specialists install the product, but miss out on handoffs, success plans, or defined ways to engage customers after implementation. The result of these siloed and tactical touch points is that customers are left to figure things out on their own. When customers suffer, you are stuck in expensive and reactive heroics.

Management consulting firm McKinsey shares that companies are often focused on customer satisfaction at the transactional level. Companies measure satisfaction and Net Promoter Scores for individual support calls, and training classes. And while they might be offering high quality services that customers love, overall satisfaction suffers when these experiences aren't aligned in a larger customer journey. McKinsey discovered that journeys correlate significantly more with overall outcomes than do touchpoints.[20] This means it's your responsibility to provide customers a coordinated and proactive approach of best practices that drive specific outcomes. McKinsey shares that the rewards of providing seamless customer journeys include higher customer and employee satisfaction, increased revenue, cost

> *When customers suffer, you are stuck in expensive and reactive heroics.*

improvements, and an enduring competitive advantage over your competitors.

It's time to turn the spotlight on your customers. Customers are the core to your financial stability and your higher profits. Their success drives your success. And the reality is that 100 percent of your customers have to be onboarded for you to be successful. When you partner with customers, learn from them, hone in on their desired outcomes, and provide clear direction and guidance, everyone benefits and makes more money. As you will see, proactive onboarding is the key to unlocking expansion along the customer journey. Start by breaking down silos. Continue with customer-facing teams working together in ways that truly impact customer retention. Build trusting and enduring relationships with customers from day one.

...journeys correlate significantly more with overall outcomes than do touchpoints.

Front loading the relationship is the recipe to higher renewals and expansions. When customers fail to launch, you never win back their business. It's onboarding that drives renewals.

When customers fail to launch, you never win back their business. It's onboarding that drives renewals.

WHAT MATTERS

» The costs associated with acquiring customers means even when you close new deals, you lose money when new customers don't renew.

» Many companies lack a comprehensive way to onboard new customers. As a result, they wait for customers to have problems and are stuck in reactive heroics trying to save problem accounts.

» Heroics don't improve customer churn rates, but they do increase employee churn rates.

» Front-loading customer relationships is the recipe to customer success.

» Providing a comprehensive customer journey increases customer satisfaction.

READY TO ONBOARD?

» Write down all the ways you and your teams use hope as a strategy to onboard and enable customers.

» Where do you use reactive heroics to engage at-risk accounts? What is that costing you?

» How are customer-facing teams stuck in silos?

» What's the first step you can take to break down silos at your company?

» What might a seamless journey for customers look like? How could this impact your company and your customers?

» How much does it cost your company to sell to new customers?

» What is the CAC ratio for every new dollar you bring in?

» How much does it cost your company to engage existing customers?

» How long does it take to break even on a new customer?

PART 2

The Six Stages of Orchestrated Onboarding

CHAPTER 3

The Orchestrated Onboarding Framework

Of course, we all want the customer to succeed. Why is that so difficult? Because it requires collaboration and cooperation across teams and people. It requires strategy and execution—not hope. It requires orchestration.

The Orchestrated Onboarding framework

The Orchestrated Onboarding framework is a cross-functional approach to customer onboarding and enablement. I call it orchestrated because it involves organizing and planning something that is complicated to achieve a desired or maximum effect.

Like a musician who picks up and plays every instrument in the orchestra during a performance, I see CSMs frantically attempt to make customers happy—all on their own. This results in a confusing and disjointed relationship with new accounts from the start, just like the clanging you hear when orchestras aren't finely tuned. However, when customer-facing roles each play their own instrument, together they provide a cohesive and harmonious arrangement. This is what customers want and this is where orchestration comes in.

Onboarding is the action or process of familiarizing new customers with your products and your services. It is the critical period after the deal closes when new customers must be guided to success. This is also the time when customers are most interested in making a difference with your product. Onboarding begins before the deal closes and may last for days or months, depending on your product. Whether it takes 90 seconds or 90 weeks, onboarding is the key to building trusting and enduring relationships with your customers.

When you use the Orchestrated Onboarding framework, you no longer feature solo artists. Instead, you have a group effort, where everyone knows the score, and everyone plays their parts. You bring coherence and harmony to the customer experience, regardless of who owns the onboarding process. No matter who is conducting—whether CSMs or onboarding specialists—they align with customer-facing teams in an orchestrated manner to provide the seamless journey customers crave.

The Orchestrated Onboarding framework includes six stages to guide customers through the initial onboarding and beyond. It's a workable process that improves communication across internal teams as well as customers. Onboarding starts during the sales cycle and continues past the product go-live to address user adoption, change management, and user turnover. It's a strategic solution to ensuring the renewal in the beginning of the customer relationship, when it most matters. Figure 7 shows a high-level overview of the Orchestrated Onboarding framework.

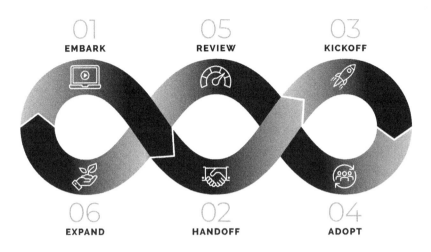

01 EMBARK
05 REVIEW
03 KICKOFF
06 EXPAND
02 HANDOFF
04 ADOPT

Figure 7: Orchestrated Onboarding™ framework

The six stages of Orchestrated Onboarding

1. **Embark.** In this stage, you sell and market the value of your Customer Success and onboarding programs, even before the deal is closed.

2. **Handoff.** Next come two handoffs: one for internal teams and another for customers, to ensure internal teams are ready for the customer journey and customer teams are ready to partner with you.

3. **Kickoff.** After handoffs, you kick off the implementation and detail all that's needed for your product to go live.

4. **Adopt.** This stage includes the actual implementation and adoption of your product and might take several weeks or even months.

5. **Review.** It's important to review progress with your customers as new account onboarding wraps up.

6. **Expand.** Keep going because there are always new users and organizations to onboard, and users need to quickly adopt the features and products that keep coming at them.

Like any good performance, you don't wow your audience overnight. It takes work and perseverance to appear effortless. Any top performer knows about the countless hours spent behind the scenes before opening night. In the same way, deliberate work and collaboration is required to deliver a seamless customer journey. In the following chapters, we'll delve into each stage of the Orchestrated Onboarding framework and use processes and templates to get started.

WHAT MATTERS

» Customer-facing teams are often siloed and, as a result, customers are not getting the appropriate help they need to be successful.

» Orchestrated means organizing and planning something that is complicated to achieve a desired or maximum effect.

» Onboarding is the action or process of familiarizing new customers with your products and your services.

» The six stages of the Orchestrated Onboarding Framework are: Embark, Handoff, Kickoff, Adopt, Review, Expand.

READY TO ONBOARD?

» Write down the stages of onboarding where you already have processes in place.

» Write down the stages of onboarding where there are gaps that need to be addressed.

» Write down all the teams currently involved in customer onboarding, as well as who might help provide a seamless journey for customers.

CHAPTER 4

Embark

Remember those neural storms going off in your customers' brains when they buy your product? In order to address the stress your new customers experience, it's vital to forge faith immediately. You do this by establishing relationships. You increase confidence when you set expectations about what happens after the sale during the sales journey. That's why the first stage of the Orchestrated Onboarding framework starts even before the deal closes.

When companies ask me how to solve issues with expectations and implementations, I tell them to start onboarding earlier. That's why Orchestrated Onboarding launches with the **Embark** stage. The purpose of this stage, which starts during the sales journey, is to help buyers understand the journey ahead of them. During Embark you start with the big picture and stay strategic. The components of the Embark stage allow you to provide continuity from the buyer journey to the customer journey, which is what's needed to establish trust. During Embark, you also sell the value of onboarding and the Customer Success services you provide customers. Then you capture important details to embark new customers in their tailored success plan.

Trust: The missing piece of customer onboarding

Sales reps are great at building relationships with buyers. Trusting relationships are a huge component of the buyer decision, and the messages buyers receive during the sales journey impact how their customer journey begins. Unfortunately, most companies throw all that relationship collateral down the drain when they win the deal. That's why the Embark stage is so important. When you start onboarding before the contract is signed, you combat the challenges of first impressions, buyer's remorse, and prospection. You quiet the neural networks of your new customers and you build trusting and enduring relationships that last. Then you continue to instill confidence in new customers during the Handoff stage, which we'll discuss in the next chapter.

> ...most companies throw all that relationship collateral down the drain when they win the deal.

Sell the value

It's important to provide value even before you win a customer. You do this by sharing the merits of your onboarding and Customer Success services during the sales cycle. When the deal nears closing, generally in the last couple of sales stages, it's a good idea to acquaint customers with the specifics about the onboarding program. This is the time to introduce the teams that guide customers to success. How you do this is covered in this chapter and the next.

I get the most push back about the Embark stage, because sales teams are reluctant to bring Customer Success professionals and onboarding into the sales cycle. However, everyone wants to see the path to success. When you produce an impressive solution, you want people to know how you make their lives better. After we implemented orchestrated onboarding at Ace Analytics, we realized our Customer

Success and onboarding offerings were significant differentiators in our crowded software space. We took advantage of this to emphasize how Ace Analytics services increased the success of our customers. Most companies don't do this. They avoid mentioning anything that happens after the sale closes.

Don't keep onboarding as your best kept secret. According to customer experience expert Joey Coleman, "The best companies in the world take the customer experience offered after the sale and infuse it into marketing and sales, so the customer gets a flavor of the good things to come. This not only incentivizes prospects to sign on the dotted line, but also properly sets the expectations for what will happen after the sale."[21] Rather than startling new customers after the sale, sell the value of your customer-facing services during the buyer journey. The earlier you show your customers you know what you are doing and that you've done this before, the faster you foster trust, and the easier it will be to engage new customers quickly. Bringing onboarding into the sales cycle may even improve your deal close rates.

Don't keep onboarding as your best kept secret.

Market and sell internally and externally

Of course, if you intend to become involved with the final stages of the sales journey, you'd better get your sales team on board first. Sales reps will need to clearly articulate the value of your programs to customers and they'll require the right tools to do so. At Ace Analytics, we hired an advertising agency to help us get the word out internally and with customers. Rather than hoping customers discovered our awesome new program, we christened it with unique branding to highlight our approach. Consequently, we committed to market and sell not just our software, but our valuable onboarding and Customer Success offerings as well. We created customer-facing collateral and illuminated the value customers receive in the customer journey throughout sales calls, demos, webinars, and user conferences. We also patiently ramped up

Sales teams to make sure they could articulate the new offering. While we didn't measure whether the Customer Success program marketing efforts actually sold more Ace Analytics software, we saw this did profoundly affect customer expectations before the deal closed. We were delighted to see new accounts ready to dive in and partner with our Customer Success teams from day one.

Selling the value of your onboarding programs is so important, Chapter Fourteen is dedicated to this. The emphasis here is to market your new products both to internal teams, especially sales, and to prospective customers to gain traction and adoption before the deal even closes.

Set expectations with success plans

I worked with a company that provides a learning management system. One of the company's customers told me it was challenging to migrate from their existing platform to the company's platform. After battling on their own with an aggressive go-live date, they were dismayed to discover an implementation package was available that would have made their lives easier. They told me they would have gladly paid extra for the assistance but didn't know it was available. In this situation, a success plan would have immediately captured the need for additional expertise. Success plans guarantee a smooth onboarding and implementation for both you and your customers.

What is a success plan?

A success plan is a single place to capture customer goals and your plan for reaching them. The plan is a document that includes best practices and quick wins, while addressing gaps and risks. It's similar to an orchestral score—a document that shows what is played by each instrument in the orchestra. It helps the conductor know which instruments will contribute at any time, so they can bring them together for a seamless experience.

> *A success plan is a single place to capture customer goals and your plan for reaching them.*

Share the success plan with customers to gain agreement on the big picture before you get stuck in the weeds of configuring, integrating, and customizing. Most importantly, success plans provide a place to address concerns and risks that might throw the project off the rails. The IT management firm ServiceSource emphasizes, "An effective Customer Success Plan mitigates potential problems with onboarding, adoption, and operations, and it provides everyone with a big-picture perspective."[22]

Capturing customer needs and expectations upfront keeps Customer Success and implementation teams from getting off to a rocky start at a time when it's most important to make a positive difference with customers. Success plans help you avoid situations, such as trying to onboard new customers only to find sales reps didn't include crucial services like training and consulting. Success plans also address those situations where new accounts don't have the right roles in place to be successful with your product. Unfortunately, nearly 70 percent of the respondents in the *2020 Customer Onboarding Report* do not provide a single place to capture customer goals and how to reach them, and they don't have a way to make this information easily accessible for internal teams and customers, as shown in Figure 8.

Success Plans

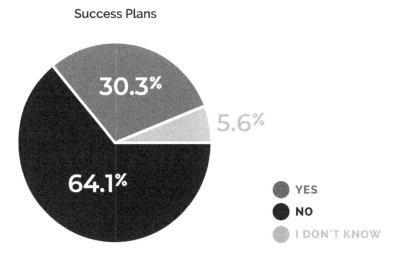

Figure 8: 2020 Customer Onboarding Report: Do you provide a single place to capture customer goals and how to reach them, accessible for both internal teams and customers?

When to create a success plan

You might wonder why success plans are included in the Embark stage. Introducing these plans before the deal closes allows you to capture the important information customers convey to sales teams and to ensure appropriate services are included in the deal. Customers don't want to push a contract through legal for approval only to find out at the kickoff meeting two weeks later that they need another sum to cover services the sale rep never mentioned. The earlier you start the success plan, the more likely sales teams will determine when a prospect requires consulting services and training so they can include the appropriate services in the deal. Also, if you want to recognize revenue the moment the deal closes, it's critical to capture everything you need in the success plan.

The Sales Engineer or Sales Consultant is a great person to populate the success plan during the sales cycle. That's because they have a good understanding of customer goals and objectives, as well as the technical requirements. When the deal closes, the success plan is transferred from the pre-sales team to the post-sales team. The sales team should review what is captured in the success plan with the CSM during the internal handoff meeting, which is covered in the next chapter. The success plan then should live in a place where it can be easily accessed by all the customer-facing teams and updated regularly.

How to create a success plan

The success plan contains information to help new accounts reach their goals and includes the following sections:

High-level **overview** of the customer

Desired **business outcomes**

Details of **what was purchased**, including services

Overview of **the implementation plan,** including quick wins (we'll cover quick wins in Chapter Eleven)

- *This is not the full implementation project plan*

Roles and responsibilities for both your company and the customer, so you both know who is involved in onboarding, implementation, and adoption

- *Capturing additional contacts beyond the buyer and the champion helps you engage accounts better*

Resources to work on the project

- *Explore whether the customer has the right team and tools in place to be successful*
- *If not, immediately address this with the buyer and stakeholders, even before the deal is done*

Training required, since this is a critical component of successful onboarding and adoption

- *Including a section for training in the success plan is a good reminder for both sales reps and customers to include it in the deal and not leave it as an afterthought*

Services are also critical, so include the right package for this account in the success plan and in the deal

Gaps and risks and the action items to address them

Sign-off by the stakeholder

Addressing gaps and risks with buyers and stakeholders during the sales cycle and the Handoff keeps customers accountable for their contribution to a successful go-live and beyond. My clients' customers tell me they want to be held accountable, so provide them the right information up front. A thorough success plan provides the transparency to start on a proactive cadence with new customers.

Success plan template

Use the template available at **OrchestratedOnboarding.com** to build your success plan.

What to do with your success plan

Once you have a success plan in place, what do you do with it? First, this is a customer-facing document, so make it look appealing. While it would be ideal to track success plan details in a customized object in your CRM or in a Customer Success platform that spits out a gorgeous report, it's fine to start with a basic document. That's what I use when I start engagements with my clients. Add your company logo and your customer logo, just like in the template, then attach it to the account record in your CRM or CS platform. Whatever you do, make sure you don't just send a blank success plan off to your customers for them to fill out. Working through the success plan together fosters the beginning of a partnership with new customers. To illustrate, the team at a company that provides large event and venue management software shared, "We've been using the success plans and they really 'upped our game.' Our customers get tangible wins and they see us as true consultants now."

The success plan commences during the Embark stage to capture what the sales teams know about customer requirements, goals, and resources. Then continue working with the success plan during the Handoff stage for the post-sales team to validate what you know about the new account. When goals, roles and responsibilities, timelines, and risks are documented and signed-off, customer accountability is improved and you have a much greater chance of a successful onboarding and implementation.

The Embark stage sets up your teams and your customers for productive onboarding and implementation. Begin building loyal relationships, sell the value of your impactful onboarding and Customer Success programs, and establish a framework of accountability and transparency with success plans. Once you've set the foundation in Embark, you and your customers are ready for the Handoff stage.

WHAT MATTERS

» Continuity from the buyer journey to the customer journey builds trust and keeps customers accountable.

» It's important to sell and market the value of your onboarding and Customer Success programs along with your software to build traction and to gain adoption.

» Marketing and selling efforts are essential to onboard both internal teams and prospects in this new strategic approach.

» A success plan is a single place to capture customer goals and your plan for reaching them. It is a document that includes best practices, quick wins, and addresses gaps and risks.

» Starting a success plan during the buyer journey captures customer requirements for internal teams and keeps customers accountable during the customer journey.

READY TO ONBOARD?

» Where does your Customer Success and onboarding currently program begin?

» Do you currently capture customer requirements in a success plan?

CHAPTER 5

Handoff

Saying the same thing over and over to multiple people is no way to start a new relationship.

"The rude and jarring experience as an individual transitions from prospect to customer is exacerbated by the complete lack of a handoff,[23] shares Joey Coleman, as he highlights the problem when customers are transferred from Sales to Customer Success. Without handoffs, CSMs rarely access the critical information shared with sales teams, leaving customers to pick up the slack. Customers are annoyed and frustrated to explain their goals and requirements repeatedly.

Once an account embarks on the journey of working together, the next stage in Orchestrated Onboarding is **Handoff**. Holding and nailing handoff meetings is a vital way to engage your customers immediately. You might notice the plural *handoff meetings*. While most companies talk about the singular handoff from Sales to Customer Success, the *two* handoffs in Orchestrated Onboarding set you up to get on track quickly. This stage includes an internal handoff meeting, as well as the customer handoff. The second stage of Orchestrated Onboarding continues the trust you built during the Embark stage while pulling the internal and customer teams together for a common purpose.

Companies are in desperate need of handoffs and alignment with internal teams and customers. Internally, you need orchestration and collaboration between sales and Customer Success. If sales reps act like soloists, telling customers only what they want to hear and signing contracts with anyone willing to give them money, who's left dealing with unrealistic expectations? The Support and Customer Success teams, of course. They have a rough time conveying the reality of what their products can and can't do, and then they pull heroics to keep these accounts alive. The Handoff stage prevents these soloists from running away with the performance. It keeps everyone playing from the same score. When you fail to align the teams on the customer side, they end up lost and confused. They don't understand what was purchased and why. They're surprised and overwhelmed when they're suddenly swarmed by CSMs, onboarding specialists, implementations teams, and project plans.

...the two handoffs in Orchestrated Onboarding set you up to get on track quickly.

Onboarding would get pretty ugly at Ace Analytics before we redesigned our onboarding process. Jumping directly from the signed contract into a long implementation cycle, we made no effort to provide continuity from the buyer journey to the customer journey, to associate with internal teams, or to develop any connection with the users in new accounts. The Ace Analytics product was technically complex. Internal and customer teams were quickly ensnared in frustrating efforts, such as importing the right data, accurately defining database fields, and the difficult task of integrating the Ace product with the customer's own software. On top of that, we were in the dark when it came to business objectives and success metrics: they were never discussed with anyone beyond the sales rep. Many companies have these same challenges. If this scenario sounds familiar, you'll love what the Handoff stage does to set you up for success.

If you don't completely hand off customer relationships from Sales to Customer Success teams at your company, think of the Handoff stage as an alignment stage. You align internal teams to get them tuned up for the important work of onboarding, and then align customer teams to prepare them for implementing and using your product.

The internal handoff

Customers tell me how frustrating it is to recount the same information with the pre-sales team, the onboarding team, the Customer Success team, and the Support team. Customer Success expert Lincoln Murphy emphasizes, "One of the things that customers hate more than anything else is having to answer the same question after the sales deal is done, that they answered two to three times during the sales process."[24] That's why the internal handoff is so important. It's when internal teams gain alignment over new accounts.

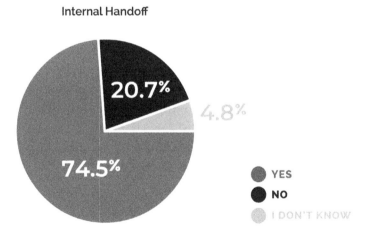

Internal Handoff

20.7%
4.8%
74.5%

● YES
● NO
● I DON'T KNOW

Figure 9: 2020 Customer Onboarding Report - Do pre-sales teams and post-sales teams meet when a new deal closes to share information about the new account?

Handoffs sustain the momentum gained before the deal closes by loading the CSM or the account owner with the information the new customer entrusts to sales reps. Nearly 75 percent of the companies in the *2020 Customer Onboarding Report* indicate they currently include an internal handoff to share information about the new account, as shown in Figure 9. This is great news. One caveat is that even though handoffs are a defined part of the Customer Success process, many companies end up not holding them because sales reps are too busy selling to the next prospect. Internal handoffs are effective only when they happen consistently. Take full advantage of the best practices in this chapter to improve your internal handoffs and to provide the continuity new customers crave.

Handoffs sustain the momentum gained before the deal closes by loading the CSM or the account owner with the information the new customer entrusts to sales reps.

Too often, when preparing for a new account, CSMs simply review the opportunity details in the CRM or other tool used to track opportunity and account information. While learning the names and purchase details of contacts is helpful, data in fields is not enough to build a meaningful relationship with new customers. Sometimes the anecdotal information that makes or breaks a relationship isn't logged in a specific field in a CRM. That's why it's necessary for the sales rep to communicate the nuances of the relationship—including concerns, personalities, and other subjective information—to the post-sales team. Sharing this knowledge gives CSMs a chance to quickly uncover issues unique to this account.

Depending on your sales cycle and your product, the internal handoff happens either before or just after the deal closes. Since sales reps are so focused on the next sale, I advocate having the CSM take the responsibility to schedule the internal handoff with the sales team and make sure it happens. To do so, the CSM and/or CS managers need insights into the pipeline so that they know which deals are about to close.

Before attending the handoff meeting, the CSM reviews what the new customer purchased and details about the account in the CRM. In order for this to work, it's necessary that sales teams capture the right details in the right places. Otherwise, CSMs are stuck trying to pull this information out of sales reps, or, even worse, asking the customer for the information. This is also the time to review what's been captured in the success plan.

Below is an overview for how to prepare for the internal handoff meeting. You can access all the Handoff resources online at **OrchestratedOnboarding.com**.

Internal handoff pre-work

CS Manager tracks accounts in the pipeline and notifies the CSM of new accounts on the horizon

CSM schedules the internal handoff meeting with the sales rep

Sales rep ensures the opportunity, account details, and success plan are updated in systems and available for other teams to review

CSM reviews the success plan, account, and opportunity details to answer these questions:

- Who is the customer?
- Which products and services did they buy?
- What is their motivation for using what they purchased?
- Who are the key contacts?
- What are the terms of the sale?
- What are the customer's goals?

Internal handoff meeting

Once the pre-work is complete, it's time to schedule the internal handoff meeting. Here's a sample agenda.

Internal handoff meeting

Attendees: CSM, Onboarding lead (if appropriate), Sales Rep, Sales Engineer

Timeframe: Just before or just after the deal closes

Time needed: 45 to 60 minutes

Agenda

- Review opportunity and account details in CRM

- Review success plan

- Address any concerns and gaps

- Review whether the appropriate services are included to ensure customer is onboarded and implemented successfully

    - If not, make sure they are added to the deal before it closes

- Discuss expectations set by the pre-sales team

- Share what's needed to transfer the relationship

    - **Details** about the stakeholders, decision makers, influencers; as well as nuances about their personalities

    - **Roles and responsibilities:** Discuss the individuals the Sales team worked with during the sales cycle versus who will be engaged during onboarding and beyond

    - **Technical capabilities:** How technically savvy are the new users? Do they need hand-holding? Are they process oriented? What's the best way to engage?

- What was the most successful form of **communication** with this customer? Phone / email / weekly meetings?
- Any gotchas and pain points?
- Any timelines and commitments promised?

Internal handoff post-work

After the meeting, follow up with these essential tasks to ensure you capture important information and close loops.

Internal handoff post-work

The CSM updates the CRM and success plan with what was learned during the internal handoff

The Sales Rep schedules the customer handoff with the new account

CSM prepares the agenda for the customer handoff

The customer handoff

The customer handoff is designed to calm neural networks and to build trust with clear endings and clear beginnings. As you learned in the section on neuroscience, it's no longer appropriate to promise customers what they want during the sales cycle, and then say, "See ya!" once the deal closes. To keep new customers from dwelling in fear and remorse you need to deliver continuity and cognitive closure. The customer handoff provides the continuation to move from the established relationship to the new teams the customer will interface with moving forward.

The customer handoff is designed to calm neural networks and to build trust with clear endings and clear beginnings.

Once the internal handoff has happened, the CSM is ready to engage the new customer. Since cognitive closure is indispensable to keep new customers from spiraling into fear and regret, hold the customer handoff ideally within seven to ten days after the deal closes, or even before the close if that makes sense with your timeline.

The customer handoff is not a kickoff meeting, where you dive into implementation details: it's a handoff meeting. Kicking off the implementation comes in the next stage of the Orchestrated Onboarding framework. The purpose is of the customer handoff is to transition the relationship from the sales reps to the CSM or other post-sales teams, to provide continuity in the relationship with your company, and to align customer teams on the objectives for buying your product. I am heartened to see that nearly 70 percent of companies in the *2020 Customer Onboarding Report* do meet with teams of new customers to make sure buyers and users are aligned on the purchase objectives, as shown in Figure 10.

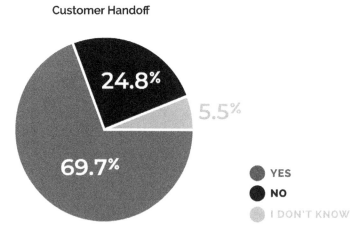

Customer Handoff

24.8%

5.5%

69.7%

● YES
● NO
● I DON'T KNOW

Figure 10: 2020 Customer Onboarding Report - Do you meet with new customer's teams to make sure their buyers and users are aligned on the purchase objectives?

The customer handoff eliminates the problem of the customer team being in the dark about what's going to happen. Implementations usually stall out or never start because customer teams have no idea what was purchased and why. They have no bandwidth to join forces with CSMs and consultants to migrate, implement, and go live. The customer handoff ensures folks who will deploy and use your solution know why it's been purchased and the problems it is meant to solve. It gives them a heads-up to know what's coming.

The customer handoff is especially important when your company works with accounts where the people who buy your product are not the ones using it. You don't want the buyer or someone in procurement acquiring your tool and then forcing it on users who have no idea why it was purchased. This is exactly what happened at one company I worked with. Their software improves patient check-ins and verifies patient insurance eligibility for medical practices. This software is usually purchased by a buyer or stakeholder of several medical practices. When the teams at my client company reach out to each medical practice to start onboarding, the people with whom they engage are usually in the dark. That's why we baked in a "client alignment" meeting during the Handoff stage of new customer onboarding. At this meeting, there is time for the stakeholder to share with their teams what was purchased and why, for teams to see a demo of the solution, and to ask questions— all before the kickoff meeting. This helps move the onboarding and implementation forward smoothly.

During the customer handoff meeting, go over the success plan together. This provides the opportunity to not just refine the desired goals and outcomes, but to also capture roles and responsibilities, project timelines, and dependencies. Customer Success leader Natalie Macks emphasizes, "Knowing what the customer expects as an outcome is key. The expectation may have shifted from when they first started talking with the salesperson, so it is critical for CSMs to ask customers, point blank, what business outcomes they expect from the solution or product."[25]

Take advantage of having the business sponsor in the meeting to highlight the gaps and risks which could impact or derail this project. The sponsor may need to address a lack of resources or services. For example, your team may identify the need for a data analyst or a dedicated system administrator in order to more easily reach their goals, or you might highlight a managed services package where you provide those roles for them. The new customer may possibly need to purchase and install hardware, which will impact the implementation timeline. This is also a good time to emphasize the need for training for end users. Addressing these issues up front increases the success of implementations. I hold an alignment meeting with my client teams before we kick off a project to make sure everyone's on the same page. We review the success plan together and always find ways to improve it. Working together goes much more smoothly when we take the time to align and review the goals and risks.

Below is a sample script for how you might address risks and gaps:

We spoke about a Q1 go-live date. This is achievable but will depend on adjusting the scope of the project and bringing your staff quickly up-to-speed on Ace products. As a result, we recommend the following, as detailed in your success plan:

Take the administrator classes we recommend.

Purchase the Quickstart Professional Services package to accelerate integrations, customizations, and the overall implementation.

Add a data analyst to your staff to improve data insights or purchase the Data Analyst Managed Services subscription.

Customer handoff pre-work

Remember the power that first impressions have on relationships? While it might seem trivial, small talk is an important way to build a good first impression. In fact, research shows that small talk helps build trust, which is just what you need when starting new relationships. Do your homework to learn about the people with whom you partner at every new customer. I prepare for meetings by checking LinkedIn for common connections and interests, as well as where my new contacts were educated and where they currently live. I use this information to get the conversation started. For example, in preparing for a meeting, I noticed my contact's LinkedIn profile showed an image of him hanging out on the top of Half Dome, the legendary granite dome in the east end of Yosemite Valley. Since I had also hiked Half Dome, I started the conversation discussing our shared passion.

A thorough internal handoff prepares you for a promising customer handoff, so be sure to complete all aspects of the internal handoff before you meet with new customers. If you start a success plan during the sales cycle, then prepare to share it with customers during the handoff meeting.

Since the purpose of the customer handoff is to gain consensus about customer objectives, think through who to invite to the meeting. It's critical for the customer's executive sponsor to be included.

Consider the following as you prepare for the customer handoff.

Customer handoff pre-work

Meeting participants:

- **Customer team:** The executive sponsor/decision maker, the project lead, implementation lead and team (if appropriate).
- **Your team:** Sales rep, sales engineer (if needed); CSM, head of Customer Success (if your customer is a key account); implementation lead (if appropriate).

Conversation starters: Prepare to connect with each person with whom you will be meeting by looking up their LinkedIn profiles.

Timing: Hold the customer handoff meeting as soon as possible so you don't leave customers hanging.

Success plan: Update the success plan with everything you know from the pre-sales journey and send a copy of the plan to attendees before the meeting, so they are ready to discuss and update the plan.

Agenda: Keep the customer handoff meeting short and sweet. Since it's a handoff, and you're not diving into implementation details just yet, 30 to 45 minutes is plenty of time. Prior to the meeting, provide all attendees an agenda so they know what will be discussed. See the sample agenda below.

Customer handoff meeting

The sales rep begins the customer handoff meeting, since they're already established as the trusted person in the account relationship. Including the sales team also gives customers the chance to transition away from the team with whom they've worked over the previous months and provides cognitive closure to the buyer journey. After the post-sales teams are introduced, the sales rep passes the baton to the CSM, and positions the CSM as the new strategic advisor with the account moving forward. Once this handoff has taken place, the CSM takes the lead with the agenda for the rest of the meeting. They review the new customer's goals and objectives in order to validate and refine what they already know.

Customer handoff agenda

Introductions

- **Sales Rep** kicks off the meeting and then introduces the CSM into the relationship and how they will lead things moving forward.

- **CSM** introduces themselves and connects with the people in the meeting.

- Each attendee introduces themselves, and shares their roles and responsibilities.

Confirm those points of contact within the account with whom the CSM will engage moving forward.

Review, validate, and update the success plan, making sure customer teams are aligned with what was determined during pre-sales.

- Discuss and clarify business objectives for the product purchase and implementation.

- Define roles and responsibilities.

- Review the timeline, next steps, and who is to be involved.

- Address risks, gaps, and concerns.

- Understand what matters to the customer and how they will measure success.

- Help the customer understand where they are accountable, and how that will be tracked.

Schedule the project kickoff meeting with the implementation teams.

Determine and schedule the meeting cadence moving forward.

Schedule the first business review while you have the business sponsor on the call to make sure they attend that review.

Customer handoff post-work

Follow up the customer handoff meeting with the appropriate tasks, which might include the following:

Customer handoff post-work

Update the success plan with what you learned during the customer handoff.

Send the updated success plan to the customer sponsor and teams to sign off.

Schedule meetings with customers teams.

Bonus: Send a handwritten card and small gift.

I worked with a company that provides software for drug trials. They created awesome documents that captured all the new customer requirements. Unfortunately, they were archived in a SharePoint folder somewhere and were never looked at again. Don't let that happen to you and to your customers. After the customer handoff, have the business sponsor sign-off on the plan to confirm they understand what's been agreed upon and the risks addressed. Then, provide access or copies of the agreed plan to customer teams and to internal teams. Success plans are living documents, so keep them handy and update them along the journey. Save each version as a new copy to keep a record of what was originally agreed upon, then leverage this valuable record and track progress during business review meetings.

The Handoff stage is an important part of the Orchestrated Onboarding framework because it establishes relationships and it builds trust. Nailing the handoffs set up you and your customers for success. You establish the basis of a trusting relationship, set up a working partnership with clear goals and a communication plan, address risks and concerns, and determine how you both are accountable.

The **internal handoff** prepares you and your teams to handle the account moving forward. The **customer handoff** is beneficial for both internal teams and customer teams. It ensures the trusted party—the sales team—is interested in the customer's success by introducing the CSM and post-sales teams into the relationship. This extends the trust already established within the account to the new teams, allowing new customers to quiet any lurking buyer's remorse, fear, and doubt, so they can relax and trust they are in good hands. After you hold two handoffs, then you finally get to kick off the implementation in the following stage of Orchestrated Onboarding, which we'll discuss in the next chapter.

Success plans are living documents, so keep them handy and update them along the journey.

WHAT MATTERS

» The handoff stage starts with the internal handoff to transition the account ownership from the sales teams to the Customer Success teams.

» The customer handoff transitions the customer relationship and also aligns customer teams on how to proceed with your product.

READY TO ONBOARD?

» Do you currently have an internal handoff? What could be improved in the process?

» Do you currently have a customer handoff? Is it really a consulting kickoff meeting? How could you improve the customer handoff?

» How might you provide access to success plans that continue to change as the customer moves through their journey with you?

CHAPTER 6

Kickoff

You've completed the handoffs? What happens next? Do you throw the customers into the weeds with a bunch of supporting technical documentation? I've seen that happen before: Customers dive deep into the undergrowth, get tangled up, then seek a lifeline from Customer Support. When customers are left to figure things out on their own, neuroscience tells us they make up stories about what's going on, which are usually worst-case scenarios. That's why the **Kickoff** stage is so critical.

The Kickoff stage of the Orchestrated Onboarding framework keeps customers from getting lost, prevents excess support tickets, and dodges buyer's remorse. The purpose of the Kickoff stage is to provide a clear structure for how to work together, including milestones, deliverables, quick wins, and customer accountability. Don't get tempted to roll the Handoff and the Kickoff stages into one to "save time." While the Handoff stage transitions the relationship from the pre-sales to the post-sales teams, the Kickoff stage shifts focus from big picture strategy to the tactics of onboarding and implementation. During Kickoff, you'll get specific about how to reach the goals and objectives you captured and validated in the success plan during the customer handoff. The Kickoff also sets the tone for progressing through the Adopt, Review, and Expand stages and beyond. Many of the components of those stages are set up in the Kickoff stage. You'll want to cover these chapters to ensure you deliver a robust kickoff.

Milestones, deliverables, and accountability

Kickoff covers how you make the success plan a reality. You'll clarify how customers are to be involved with you and your teams. You'll address where they're accountable, how you'll track their accountability, what milestones and deliverables are coming, and discuss any blockers that need to be removed or managed.

You'll want to emphasize the role your customers play in achieving their own success.[26] The Kickoff often involves project plans for implementation and adoption, which might be delivered through sophisticated onboarding software, project management tools, or simple spreadsheets. Clearly map out the phases of implementation, the roles and their responsibilities, and all the details and timelines needed. I like to include visuals to help users process all this information more easily. We'll discuss this in more detail in Chapter Fifteen. The implementation and services teams most likely build out these plans, which is why you should include them during the Kickoff stage as needed. Then share the plan with customers, so they know how their journey begins, with whom they are to associate and when, and the direction in which they're headed.

The kickoff meeting

The kickoff meeting is centered on project plans, roles, responsibilities, timelines, and deliverables.

Before the kickoff meeting, ensure you take care of the important pre-work covered below. All Kickoff resources are available at **OrchestratedOnboarding.com**

Kickoff Pre-work

Timing: Within five to ten business days after the customer handoff meeting.

Have the CSM review the success plan.

Create a shared project plan and assets to review with the customer.
- *Include details about implementation, consulting services, adoption, and training; how they fit together, and who does what and when.*

Determine how to track accountability and timelines for both your teams and the customer's teams.

Consider whether the customer has required actions before the kickoff meeting. If so, communicate them clearly.
- *For example, it might be helpful for the customer to have a payment gateway plan in place before you meet.*

Invite attendees and send the agenda.

Because the Kickoff centers on project plans, roles, responsibilities, timelines, and deliverables, invite those who are ready to roll up their sleeves and dive into the details. Most likely this includes the team leads on the customer side—you don't need to include the business sponsors. It's good practice to have the CSM lead the kickoff meeting, even when other teams like onboarding and implementation are involved. This is to cement the relationships with the people who attended the handoff meeting.

Kickoff Meeting Overview

Internal attendees: CSM, onboarding and implementation team leads, as needed

Customer attendees: Project lead, team members, as needed

Time needed: 60 minutes

Agenda

- Introduce members of customer and company teams; share locations, roles, and an interesting fact about yourselves.
- Review the success plan and fine tune, if needed.
- Review the process for working together to onboard and implement your product.
- Provide an overview of onboarding, implementation, consulting, and training services, and how they fit together.
- Review the project plan, timeline, and dependencies.
- Discuss roles and responsibilities. Provide user flows and swim lanes, if appropriate.
- Cover what the customer is responsible for and how that will be tracked.
- Discuss meeting cadence (how often you will meet).
- Review how to log support tickets, if appropriate.
- Review how to access such resources as knowledge articles, how-to videos, self-paced training, and documentation.
- Discuss next steps and note action items.

The kickoff meeting postwork

Follow up with the customer immediately.

Send an email that provides access to all the assets you discussed.

Update the project plan; share it with the new customer teams.

Let everyone know their action items.

Tell them when you will next meet. This proactive step shows the new customer you are in charge, and it also sets those positive first impressions, which are so important.

A well-defined Kickoff is like a well-lit road with signposts pointing customers in the right direction. Customers aren't left to find the right path on their own, dwell in worry and doubt, and then call you when they have a problem. Instead, you provide a clear framework for how to work together to reach their goals. Customers relax because they don't have to figure anything out on their own. In the next chapter, we'll dive into the meat and potatoes of onboarding—the Adopt stage.

A well-defined Kickoff is like a well-lit road with signposts pointing customers in the right direction.

WHAT MATTERS

» The Kickoff stage is unique from the Handoff stage.

» While the Handoff is about relationships, building trust, and the big picture goals and outcomes, the Kickoff stage is about the details of implementation and adoption.

READY TO ONBOARD?

» How do you currently address the Kickoff stage at your company? How could you improve it?

» How do you prepare for the kickoff meeting?

CHAPTER 7

Adopt

Could you imagine retaining customers that don't ever adopt your product? Without adoption, your customers don't have a product to use, and you don't have a license to renew. Adoption occurs when your users take up and use the implemented and customized product. It's important because your product quickly becomes shelfware if it's not installed correctly or users don't know how to properly use it.

The **Adopt** stage includes such implementation phases as customizing, integrating, and launching your product or platform. It also addresses user onboarding and enablement, so the customer's people know how to use your product. Depending on the industries and user types with whom you work, this stage also includes change management, which is a must-have for end user adoption. Because the Adopt stage includes multiple components, it's the longest stage of the Orchestrated Onboarding framework besides the Expand stage—it may last weeks or possibly even months. I prefer incorporating quick wins into the Adopt stage to drive customers to rapid value, even during long

> *The Adopt stage includes such implementation phases as customizing, integrating, and launching your product or platform.*

implementations. We'll talk about quick wins in Chapter Eleven. The Adopt stage begins after both the customer handoff meeting (where teams align on the big picture) and after the kickoff meeting (where everyone involved aligns on the implementation and adoption plan).

Many companies equate onboarding with implementation. This is a mistake. As you now know, onboarding starts even before the deal closes to start building trusting relationships with new customers. Rather than having a laser focus on the checklists and technical details, include the big picture of the timelines, roles and responsibilities, and accountabilities during the Adopt stage to ensure a greater success than just going live with your product.

Creating a seamless journey

The Adopt stage is where customer-facing services come together to help customers implement and embrace your product. Services like consulting, support, and training are traditional ways of helping companies customize, integrate, and use your product. While these services have been around much longer than the Customer Success function, they often operate as soloists, focused on their task at hand rather than the larger customer journey. When it comes to seamless customer journeys, soloists can't pull this off—you need orchestration. What's unique in the Orchestrated Onboarding framework is the focus on the customer and their experience, rather than the particular service being delivered at any given time. Customers want a seamless experience, and that means services teams must now band together to provide what customers want.

I considered breaking the Adopt stage into implementation and adoption, but merging them together makes the journey more effective. You don't install, configure, and customize products for their own sake. The point is to deploy products that make people's lives better. That means users need a product to which they can relate and know how to use. Another reason to roll implementation, enablement, and change management into one stage is that new customers ideally interact with several teams as they work through all these steps. I specify ideally, because it's important that CSMs don't single-handedly manage all these important functions. Since Orchestrated Onboarding is a team effort, design a cross-functional journey where customers interact with the right team at the right time.

It's important to emphasize that services provided during the Adopt stage are each unique and robust disciplines. Professionals usually specialize as a Professional Services Consultant, an instructional designer, or an instructor. Change management is also a unique specialty. While this chapter covers a brief overview of each of these areas, this is by no means comprehensive coverage of what's needed to implement products and to develop and deliver courses. Instead, the consideration for onboarding is how these functions work together to provide effectual and seamless journeys for customers. In order to foster the collaboration required, more companies are pulling these customer-facing teams together under one Customer Success organization.

Implementation

Implementing (or deploying) your product means making it active and effective for your customers. It encompasses post-sale processes that you may or may not have worked through with your customers during the Adopt stage to build, fit, or alter your product to their specifications. Customers usually cooperate with professional services consultants and support agents during implementation, on some or all of these activities:

- Analyzing requirements
- Migrating data
- Installing software and hardware
- Configuring and customizing the software and hardware
- Adding custom fields
- Embedding software into customer applications
- Connecting to the appropriate data sources and systems customers already have in place

- Running tests
- Branding
- Setting up sandbox and production environments
- Conducting user acceptance testing

Implementation takes anywhere from a few moments to several months, depending on the complexity of your product and the number of customizations and integrations needed on the customer side. After deployment, you have the opportunity to launch your product to your customer. Launch is when the software goes live and is released to the users with the customization and integrations (mostly) working.

Enablement

Enablement, or educating your customers, is the action of preparing each user type to do their job using your product. Enablement might include self-paced courses, instructor-led courses, or a combination of both. This is such an important component of both user and customer success that Chapter Thirteen is dedicated to this topic. Many companies utilize CSMs to fulfill this important task, but I advise against that. Instead, create a dedicated person or team to enable your customers.

Implementation and enablement are usually two distinct components of onboarding that don't overlap, but I encourage you to blend them. They're more powerful when they work in harmony. When customers take the appropriate courses before consultants engage, implementation tends to roll out more smoothly and quickly. I've experienced this with many organizations. Customer teams have a better grasp of the product and are ready to focus on their unique customizations. They don't have to figure out the new software while also defining implementation requirements with consultants. In addition, this allows consultants to make use of their deep technical expertise to focus on unique use cases, instead of walking through basic overviews of the product at the beginning of every engagement. Bringing implementation and enablement in tune with each other keeps consultants engaged and challenged while providing customers better value.

If you have a highly technical product, you might structure your consulting agreement to train the customer's developers before you begin the consulting work. We did that at Ace Analytics and found developers grasped the parameters that could be customized, integrated, and implemented after receiving a technical overview of the Ace product during training. Ace courses helped clarify what could be accomplished during the consulting engagement, and

> *Implementation and enablement are more powerful when they work in harmony.*

customers aligned their requirements with the reality of the platform straightaway. Ace Analytics also found new customers logged far fewer support tickets during the implementation with this approach.

As customizations were finalized and the product neared launch, we next looped in the account's administrators. Their jobs were to set up users in the new system and to define roles and responsibilities for the organization. We made sure to cover all they needed to do this well in the administrator courses. Finally, we delivered end user training at or near the go live date to ensure the best user retention. Figure 11 shows how Ace Analytics blended the implementation and enablement components to create a seamless and productive customer experience throughout the Adopt stage.

DEVELOPER TRAINING ⇒ CONSULTING ⇒ ADMIN TRAINING ⇒ PRODUCT GO LIVE ⇒ END USER TRAINING

Figure 11: Blending implementation and enablement services

Once this blended approach was mapped out, Ace Analytics trained internal teams to guide customers along the defined path. That way, when a customer wanted to jump right into the consulting engagement, the head of Professional Services emphasized that developer training was required before a consultant would start the project. We baked this new approach into customer onboarding. Most importantly, we bundled all the services customers needed to be successful into Customer Success packages and then sold this as a single package. As a customer centric organization, we guided customers down a prescriptive path. We'll explain how to do this in Chapter Fourteen.

Change management

Change management is the discipline that guides how you prepare, equip, and support customers to successfully adopt the change associated with buying your product. Change management goes beyond implementation and enablement to address changes to processes, job roles, organizational structures, and expectations.

Include change management in the Adopt stage so customers can transform their businesses, beyond simply using your product. When users don't embrace your product or adopt the changes required by the initiative that caused them to purchase your product, the account will churn. Manage change to drive adoption on three levels: the enterprise, the organization, and the individual.[27] Change management addresses the actual people at the customer, because they are the ones modifying the way they work.

Manage change to drive adoption on three levels: the enterprise, the organization, and the individual.

The two main ingredients of change management are communication and more communication. At all levels, be sure to communicate why the change is happening and the desired outcomes. Communication starts in the Embark stage and continues through the Kickoff and Adopt stages to align and engage teams and prepare them for what's coming. Explore ways to help your customers embed the new way of doing things into their existing processes. Once your product and associated new processes are rolled out, reinforce the change and reward the new behavior. For example, if business users are required to accurately complete fields in your product as part of their role, include incentives to encourage them to do so.[28]

Start with the familiar

Do you encounter resistance from end users, even when your product provides them huge value? People prefer the familiar, even when a change makes their lives better. I was surprised that most of the new users at Ace Analytics resisted the powerful analytics tools we sold in favor of what they already knew—spreadsheets. Customers loved the formulas, charts, and pivot tables they carefully built into their coveted sheets. They didn't want to relinquish them, even for a sophisticated online tool that allowed drilldowns, customizations, and instant updates for everyone to access.

Change—whether it's welcome or not—provokes fear and anxiety. Address this by starting with the familiar. At Ace Analytics, I built ways to describe our sophisticated reports in spreadsheet terms into the end user training. I helped users explore existing reports in basic ways before they built their own reports. This helped them accept the changes and absorb the learning.

Make it easy for customers to change

Depending on how much change management is required, consider providing and even selling this service to customers to help them successfully adopt your product. Work with your customer to determine the right communication vehicles to roll out your products. Deliver templates for emails, announcements, and presentations so the client doesn't have to figure this out on their own.

Clear and consistent messaging is an important part of managing change, so make it easy for customers to adopt your tools and templates to communicate with their teams. The customer handoff meeting is a great time to talk with the executive sponsor about how your product will be rolled out to users. You could supply a set of email templates with communications to send out to different teams at the beginning of the implementation—before it goes live, at launch, and at specific dates after the launch to follow up. With this type of communication, all users know what's coming and what's expected of them. Here's an example of the timing:

- Project start
- Launch minus 30 days
- Launch minus 15 days
- Launch minus 5 days
- Launch day announcement and celebration
- Follow-up every week

Change management helps both individuals and organizations successfully transition to the new way of doing things, so they will gladly use your product and reach their goals.

Avoiding "bunch ball"

While you don't want customers falling into gaps as they move between phases in the Adopt stage, or between stages of onboarding, you also don't want to play "bunch ball" with customers. Bunch ball refers to the way young children play games like soccer. Rather than each playing their respective positions, like offense, wing, or defense, everyone on the field chases the ball in a bunch, eager to kick it.

This happened at a company with whom I worked that provides drug trial software. Because they had no comprehensive way to track account details, the sales rep, CSM, consultants, and management all joined in every time someone met with the customer! Internal teams were terrified to miss anything the customer mentioned, so everyone showed up to every meeting. As you can imagine, customers were overwhelmed when they were swarmed by the company's teams on a call, and internal teams had little time to focus on their "real" jobs when they were rushing from meeting to meeting. When you make the best use of the handoffs and success plans in the Orchestrated Onboarding framework, you build transparency and trust across internal teams, so everyone can play their respective roles with customers.

The Orchestrated Onboarding framework keeps the momentum going through the Adopt stage by leveraging the success plans you've already defined. When initially creating success plans with accounts, make sure to include recommended services to ensure customers move through the Adopt stage thoroughly. For example, the success plan might highlight the need to hire or assign a dedicated developer role, then point customers to the appropriate courses. The success plan should also identify whether or not change management will be a critical part of the Adopt stage.

> *Change management helps both individuals and organizations successfully transition to the new way of doing things, so they will gladly use your product and reach their goals.*

Consider bundling the services customers need into a premium Customer Success package. The package might include consulting, training, and change management services. Chapter Fourteen covers this topic fully.

WHAT MATTERS

» Onboarding in general (and the Adopt stage in particular) encompass much more than implementing your product.

» The Adopt stage takes anywhere from a few days to several months, and incorporates implementation, enablement, and change management.

READY TO ONBOARD?

» Do you know how long it takes to implement your product?

» How are you addressing the needs for your users to learn your product?

» Explore with customers whether they would benefit from change management services.

CHAPTER 8

Review

The **Review** stage is a short but critical piece of the Orchestrated Onboarding framework. Reviews are formal and strategic discussions with stakeholders, with the goal to learn from customers. Hold the review meeting about 90 days after the kickoff. For short deployments, users might already be live and actively using your product. For long implementations, accounts might still be making their way through the Adopt stage. Regardless, it's important to stay connected with your customers and to step back from the tactics of deploying and using your product to review the original objectives and outcomes for which your customers are aiming. The Review allows you to rectify any changes needed within specific accounts, while also improving your onboarding program for all customers.

How did onboarding go?

Listening to customers is as important for your success as it is for theirs. Find out how the process is going by listening. Too often, internal teams do all the talking in meetings with customers. They are so busy running on about the number of support tickets logged, the average time to resolve support issues, usage metrics, and the product roadmap that customers don't have a chance to get a word in about what's working for them. Or not.

If you want to guarantee you never get the account stakeholders to attend another review meeting, make sure you try to sell to them during the review. While you might invite sales reps and product managers to discuss features and present the product roadmap in review meetings, the focus is still to listen, not to sell. We'll discuss the importance of listening to your customers in Chapter Ten. Rather than talking at your customers, use the Review stage to build alignment, keep customers on track with their goals, guide them to more value in your product, and learn how to improve your services and products.

Listening to customers is as important for your success as it is for theirs.

Provide value during the review

Make sure customers walk away with value from the review meeting by following best practices shared by Kristen Hayer, CEO of The Success League, in The Success League's excellent Customer Success course, *Executive Business Reviews*, which is part of the CSM Certification program.[29]

1. **Develop a standard format for sharing goals and results.**
   This prevents CSMs from recreating the wheel with every review meeting. It also means you review the same document with your customers every meeting, and over time you start to see trends to celebrate or address. The format might include the original success plan you created before the deal closed.

2. **Nothing speaks louder than metrics.**
   Arrive at review meetings armed with data that highlights successes and provides insights into challenges. Be sure to include visuals, such as graphs and reports, because our brains respond better to

visual than verbal data. Always bring more information than you
think you need, so you don't get stumped by a tough question from
leadership.

3. Be candid.
Ask your customer how they feel you have performed so far. This
gives them the chance to provide you with honest feedback and to
let you know if their expectations are being met. In turn, be sure to
share any concerns on your side. Finally, don't be afraid to tactfully
ask if you are on track to secure their contract renewal. It's always
good to gauge the temperature well in advance so you don't end up
with any surprises at the contract's end.

4. Be neutral and fact-based.
Don't try to skew results to make you or your customers look
better. Customers respect you more when you candidly share what's
working and what needs to improve.

The review meeting
Download the Review resources at **OrchestratedOnboarding.com**.

Review meeting pre-work

Take advantage of these activities to prepare for the review meeting.

Review and update the success plan. Update any objectives. Note
quick wins achieved.

Prepare metrics—including product usage, support tickets,
engagement activities, NPS, customer health score, and
benchmarking across the company's industry or similar size
companies. Anticipate what your customers want and need to know.

Research news about the company and team on their website, press releases, LinkedIn, Glassdoor, social media, Crunchbase.

Prepare the meeting slide deck, including metrics and visuals.

Create an agenda.

Procure *swag*—promotional items with your company logo, such as t-shirts, notebooks, coffee mugs, to provide during an in-person meeting, or to ship to the customer for a remote meeting, if that aligns with your company / industry.

Invite participants and send the agenda.

While you may not present everything you prepare to the customer, it's helpful to have extra information, metrics, and data in your back pocket ready for wherever the conversation might go during the meeting. During the initial review meeting while onboarding is still fresh, it's great to learn from new customers what works and what to improve in the onboarding program. That way, you can keep improving each stage of the journey and bring teams together for a harmonious customer experience.

The review meeting

The review meeting takes place about 90 days after the Kickoff.

Attendees

- Internal teams: CSM, onboarding specialist/team, product managers, sales rep, executives—as needed.
- Customer teams: business sponsor, project lead, and team members as needed.

Time needed: 90 minutes to a few hours, depending on the customer.

Agenda

Introductions: Take a moment to catch up with people you already know and to connect with those joining the meeting for the first time.

Updates: Review and update the success plan together. Go over the initial goals defined at the handoff meeting and then share the progress made against those goals. Now that you are about 90 days into the project, have goals shifted? Are there blockers that need to be discussed? Include data and metrics here as much as possible.

Wins and feedback: Take a moment to celebrate how far you have come together. If that's not the case, then determine how to partner to advance the project moving forward.

Usage and benchmarking data: Customers love to know how they compare to similar accounts, so share what's appropriate and meaningful for this account.

Best practices and recommendations: Since you provide a proactive and prescriptive approach, take the opportunity to guide the account on key areas that deliver impact for them.

Customer initiatives and roadmap: Take time to learn where your customer is focused. Are there areas where you, your products, and/ or your teams can help them progress easier, faster, more affordably?

New products and solution roadmap: Take the opportunity to briefly share what's on your product roadmap. If appropriate, invite the product manager to share this information.

Questions, answers, discussions: Make time for general discussion, to answer questions, and to address concerns.

Schedule next review meeting: Determine the ongoing review meeting cadence and who should attend. Make it your goal to finish every review meeting with the next meeting already scheduled on the calendar.

Action items and next steps: Capture all action items, next steps, their owners and dates.

Review meeting post-work

Reviews are most useful when you follow up. What did you learn in the meeting? What action items did you capture? Following up on what was discussed builds customer confidence.

Review meeting post-work

Next steps email: Email all participants with an overview of what was discussed, any decisions made, a copy of metrics and slides, details of next steps, and who is accountable.

Log action items: Enter tasks/calls to actions in the appropriate systems and assign them to owners with dates.

Thank you note: If appropriate, send a hand-written thank you note.

Mail swag: If appropriate, send the customer branded swag.

Update: Update the success and project plans with next steps, new goals, dates, owners, risks, etc.

Once the onboarding review is complete, establish a cadence for future reviews that will work for your customers and your team. Many companies call review meetings "quarterly" business reviews, but this does not mean they have to be held every three months, whether you like it or not. It's more important to have a meaningful cadence than fit a specific timeframe.

WHAT MATTERS

» The purpose of the review is to listen to customers, so allot most of the review meeting agenda to learn what's working for customers, what they would improve, and to hear about their latest initiatives and goals.

READY TO ONBOARD?

» Observe a couple review meetings and determine whether you currently do most of the talking or listening. How can you improve?

» What review meeting cadence works with your accounts?

CHAPTER 9

Expand

It happens too often. Just when a new account is finally onboarded and goes live, the customer's internal champion leaves and poaches half their team. When this occurs, you have the unexpected extra burden of onboarding and training a new set of users in existing accounts, all while ramping up an onslaught of new customers.

The reality is customer onboarding never ends. The **Expand** stage of the Orchestrated Onboarding framework addresses the ongoing need to engage existing customers. As long as users keep changing and your product keeps updating, your onboarding program needs to tackle constant change. This will sustain and increase product adoption, move customers to additional use cases in your products, and increase the lifetime value of your customers. Providing Orchestrated Onboarding for the *initial* onboarding decreases time to first value and increases customer loyalty when it's most critical. When you design an *ongoing* onboarding program, you increase product adoption, product usage, and customer engagement. This is especially

> *As long as users keep changing and your product keeps updating, your onboarding program needs to tackle constant change.*

useful if your company works primarily with a lower volume of large enterprise accounts, as the Expand stage gives a boost to keeping them involved with you.

Onboarding accounts versus users

Consider the difference between onboarding a new account versus onboarding the people who will use your software. Likely a new account includes one-off events like customizing and branding your product, integrating it with other systems, and setting a go-live date. While you celebrate when an account is officially launched, this is just the beginning of user adoption. Users are the actual people who employ your product to do their jobs. They may be end users, business users, administrators, analysts, and developers. They might use your product once a day, all day every day, or just once a year. The *2020 Customer Onboarding Report* shows that nearly 65 percent of respondents do not formally onboard new users in existing accounts, as shown in Figure 12. Since onboarding and adoption are crucial to an account's success, these organizations miss a huge opportunity to expand the use of their products with existing customers.

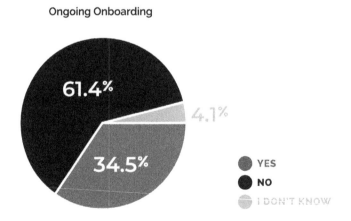

Ongoing Onboarding

61.4%
4.1%
34.5%

● YES
● NO
● I DON'T KNOW

Figure 12: 2020 Customer Onboarding Report: Do you formally onboard new users in existing accounts?

How do you deal with all the new people that need to benefit from your product but don't know how to do so? The challenge is that user turnover is high in many industries. So even when you get that first team up to speed, your new account may be at risk of churn. A LinkedIn study indicates you can expect to have up to 13 percent turnover of users each year, especially if your customers are in the technology or retail industries.[30] This means that if 100 people use your product at just one account, then 13 of them will likely leave the company by the end of the year. When you include internal changes like ongoing reorganizations, that number probably doubles. Consider the work it takes for one CSM to single-handedly try to onboard and train not just each new account they manage, but each new user in existing accounts as well. Since your CSMs don't have the bandwidth to meet this need, you risk a decline in product usage and an increase in churn when you rely on CSMs to onboard and enable all new users.

Effective customer enablement allows CSMs to be tour guides, pointing new users to training offerings rather than personally instructing each individual. Ideally, you will have a team that specializes in creating self-paced and live online courses for anyone to access at any time. Once these offerings are in place you exponentially increase the number of people who can learn to use your software without extra effort on your part. The more functional guidance you provide, the better you can guide each user type, or role, to their desired outcomes. For best results, emphasize how people do their jobs using your product, rather than giving them a friendly interface tour.[31] See Chapter Thirteen to learn how to scale customer enablement and, ultimately, Customer Success.

Onboarding existing product updates

Every time your product updates, each person using it needs to master the new features. You want customers to keep gaining value in your product, so it's important to find scalable ways to drive adoption of those new features your product teams worked so hard to roll out.

Webinars are a great way to get the message out, especially since you can record them for access on demand.

You can also create delta courses and content to get the people using your software up to speed on new product releases. Delta content focus on the differences between one release and the next, so you don't need to keep recreating the same general content for every new piece of enablement content you create. As with any new product, you want people to see value in new features and functions quickly. Keep the content pretty simple for minor product releases and invest in thorough enablement content for major releases.

Onboarding new products

New products require you to drive customers to get both initial and long-term value. Connect with the product team to build enablement content while the product is in development, then make it available as soon as the new release goes live. Be certain to include content that helps users understand why they need this new product and where it fits within your product suite or platform. When enabling people, it's always important to emphasize how it makes their lives easier and not just what the product does.

Onboarding new divisions within existing accounts

Do you sell your product into new departments within existing accounts? For example, perhaps you initially sold your product into one division of a multinational company. Now they want to expand adoption to other territories. There are important considerations to determine how the new groups need to be onboarded. Your answers to these questions determine the onboarding plan for new divisions in existing accounts:

- What are the requirements of the new division?
- Does the new organization require a separate implementation and integration?

- Do you need to customize your product for the specific needs of the new division?

- Will you onboard new users to an existing implementation or to a completely new one?

- What are the goals and outcomes of the new organization?

When expanding the number of users to an existing product implementation, focus on the needs of user onboarding and adoption. However, if each new department has different objectives that require customizations unique to their business, treat it as new account onboarding and loop back to the Handoff stage of the Orchestrated Onboarding framework. Depending on the scenario, you may want to deploy an ongoing onboarding program that addresses the requirements of each new organization. I also urge you to build out playbooks and templates to consistently and quickly onboard new divisions.

Onboarding different phases of the customer lifecycle

Rather than throwing everything about your product to users at once, it's helpful to define a customer maturity lifecycle, which details how customers adopt your product in different stages. Once you capture the path to customer maturity, your onboarding program needs to convey how you begin onboarding customers for basic use cases and then move to more complex cases as they increase their experience.

Most companies don't address customer maturity as an ongoing process. A company with a rebate management platform reasoned they should show their users how to do the most difficult task first to ensure customers would figure out the more simple things moving forward. Well, that didn't work. Instead, it caused onboarding to grind to a halt because customers were so overwhelmed.

Slow down and emphasize the basics first. For example, the first step in the journey might be to create a simple workflow. Once people in the account are comfortable with what they know and can successfully accomplish with your product, you can then guide them to create sophisticated workflows. For each step, build on their existing experience and knowledge until they increase the intricacy of their work with your product.

Another option is to start with specific modules of your product and then move to additional modules that you expose or sell along the lifecycle. Remember to draw on the original success plan you have with each account, and then onboard the parts of the product as people need them, as if they are new products. As with user adoption, start with one simple, familiar thing and build from there. This approach is transforming a CRM company with whom I work. They moved from a "you can do anything on our platform" approach to selling distinct products. Each product aligns with specific jobs to be done by roles like CEOs, sales reps, and support teams. Then they provide the appropriate training content for each role. The goal is to show wins to ensure customers achieve value over weeks, not months. When you focus on customer maturity, you increase the value your customer receives from your product, which makes them "sticky."

It's important to design the customer maturity model from the customer perspective, not from that of your company. My research into customer maturity models uncovered many examples defined in terms of what the software provider wants and needs. This includes stages like align, progress, commit, and mature—which aren't terms that inspire your customers. Take a new approach and express use cases and milestones from your customers' view-point to help them maximize the value in your product over the long term.

> *When you focus on customer maturity, you increase the value your customer receives from your product, which makes them "sticky."*

Despite your best efforts to onboard and enable new customers, the need for onboarding remains. Whether your customers are large or small, the Expand stage addresses new users in existing accounts, product updates, new products, new organizations in existing accounts, and customer maturity. Customers get continuous value from new features, new products, as well as from their new users, which increases the customer lifetime value for you.

In Part Three of this book, you'll learn the principles behind a successful onboarding program.

WHAT MATTERS

» As long as users keep changing and your product keeps updating, your onboarding program needs to tackle the constant change.

» Ongoing onboarding includes onboarding the people who use your product, new users, new product features, new products, expanding to new divisions, and higher levels of customer maturity.

READY TO ONBOARD?

» Do you currently onboard users as well as accounts?

» Write down all the different user types that need to adopt your product.

» How do you address the user turnover within existing accounts?

» How do you onboard existing users to new product releases?

» How do you onboard existing users to new products?

» How do you onboard new organizations in existing accounts? Do they require a whole new implementation?

» Have you defined a customer maturity model to guide users to more sophisticated user cases in your product?

PART 3

The Principles of Orchestrated Onboarding

CHAPTER 10
Design Thinking Principles

While some companies jump on the Customer Success bandwagon with amazing speed, most ignore their customers. It seems many teams are too busy planning and managing to consider their customers. The problem is you can't innovate without understanding your customers. Listening and empathizing, or using design thinking, are essential principles of the Orchestrated Onboarding framework, that will put you on the fast track to improving your company, selling your products, and to leading your customers to successful outcomes.

Mike Gospe, an expert Customer Advisory Board (CAB) facilitator and co-founder of the KickStart Alliance, shared his philosophy with me: "Whoever understands the customer best, wins. This means that when all products eventually become commoditized, the vendor-customer relationship will become the only relevant differentiator."[32] To illustrate this, customer experience firm Walker revealed in their *Customers 2020* report, "Empowered customers ... will demand a new level of 'customer obsession.' They will expect companies to know their business inside and out and use their knowledge to design products and services that create a 'frictionless' experience. To do this, companies must engage in a collaborative, consultative relationship with customers."[33]

When I work with companies, I often don't see much consulting and collaborating taking place. Instead, I observe leaders with their heads down analyzing churn, without ever knowing what their best customers are doing. I notice teams designing customer journeys from an internal perspective, providing ad hoc customer services, and hoping customers figure out what to do and when. Customer Success professionals harness what they learn from all the awesome content available through Customer Success articles, podcasts, webinars, meetups, and conferences, but they miss the opportunity to really learn from their own customers. When you don't know what your customers want and need, how can you define and design proactive solutions that lead to their success?

Whoever understands the customer best, wins.

The answer is to harness **design thinking** principles to listen to your users. The point of design thinking is to build programs and offerings that address the unique needs of your products and your customers. Rikke Dam and Teo Siang from the Interaction Design Foundation in Denmark share, "The Design Thinking process is iterative, flexible and focused on collaboration between designers and users, with an emphasis on bringing ideas to life based on how real users think, feel and behave." Design thinking includes a flow of stages from empathizing, to ideating, to prototyping solutions in order to build products and offerings that meet users' needs.[34] Figure 13 shows an overview of the design thinking process.

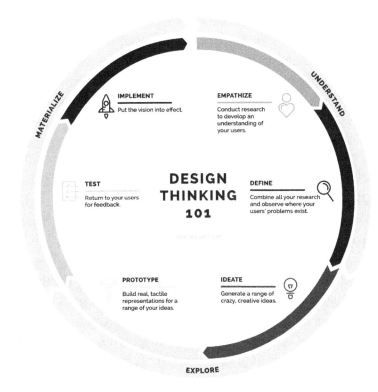

Figure 13: Design Thinking Overview from Nielson Norman Group[35]

Start with empathy

The crucial first stage of the design process is empathy. Empathy is our ability to see the world through other people's eyes. In the first stage of design thinking, your goal is to gain an empathetic understanding of the people for who you are designing solutions. You need to know the problems they are trying to solve and understand their motivations and challenges.[36] An effective onboarding strategy must include ways to empathize with your customers. Mike Gospe emphasizes, "Learning how to listen to your customers may be your most important skill. Listening requires patience and empathy. It is a sign of strength and honor, not weakness. And it requires a committed investment in nurturing long-term relationships with your best customers."[37] When

I help companies create customers for life, we focus on building empathy into the project. Listening to internal teams and to several customers reveals important information that propels innovation.

It's amazing what I learn from listening. The customers of a company that supplies digital experience management software raved about their relationship with the company. In fact, every customer I talked to declared this to be their best vendor relationship, and even a "model for other vendors." With another company that provides a learning technology platform, interviews revealed a different perspective from each customer. "The relationship with the CSM is great," gushed one customer. "There is no relationship," lamented another. While the first set of customer feedback sounds like great news, it leaves me concerned about the long-term cost of providing this white-glove treatment. The second set of customers highlights the lack of consistency and transparency in the customer-facing teams and points to gaps that need to be addressed.

An effective onboarding strategy must include ways to empathize with your customers.

The reality is that Customer Success teams are "largely stuck in a reactive mode, defined by the threat of churn," finds Mikael Blaisdell, Executive Director of the Customer Success Association.[38] A never-ending fire leaves you little time to listen to customers. Dealing with issues after they happen means one day you will wake up with a churn problem—even if you don't have one now. Organizations that are reactive don't have the time or energy to be empathetic. They avoid listening to customers. One top sales rep at Ace Analytics warned, "You're inviting trouble. Talking to customers just opens a can of worms." To move your company and our industry forward, you must engage customers in the way customers want and need to be engaged. Starting with empathy, move along the design thinking process to explore ideas and to prototype approaches with your customers.

How to listen to customers

You may assume sending out a quarterly survey to determine your Net Promoter Score (NPS) takes care of "voice of the customer" needs. However, connections and relationships are made during conversations, not surveys. In a *Harvard Business Review* article, Jamie Cleghorn and Lori Sherer identify the need to "talk with customers to understand their experience. Conduct follow-up interviews to explore their needs and sources of satisfaction and frustration, and the compromises they make in using your products and services."[39] It really does make a big difference to pick up the phone to ask how things are going. *And then listen.* At Ace Analytics, I made it a priority to call one customer a week to listen to suggestions for improvement. The conversations I had were instrumental in the innovations we built into customer-facing programs.

Once you establish the empathy principle, the next step is to build listening touchpoints along the customer journey.

To move your company and our industry forward, you must engage customers in the way customers want and need to be engaged.

Listening opportunities could include product advisory boards (PABs), customer advisory boards (CABs), user communities, networking events, user conferences, and road shows. When customers are online or in town for company and industry events, schedule a few minutes to connect for a live chat. Listen to their pain points and ask how they would fix things. Mike Gospe emphasized to me the importance of coordinating the listening points. "When building a voice-of-the-customer program, it's important to use the right tool for the right job. In other words, you want to ask the right questions to the right individuals, from the right customers, who can actually answer your question. Nothing is more wasteful and confusing than asking the right question to the wrong customers."[40]

Be careful of skewing what you learn by listening to just a handful of customers. Both Walker and Harvard emphasize the need to engage a diverse group of customers on your listening journey: "Make sure to conduct interviews in a spectrum of customer organizations, especially those at the leading edge of growth in their industries. Avoid using an existing customer panel or user group, whose members might say what they think you want to hear. And consider conducting the interviews through a neutral third party, because customers are more likely to provide honest feedback to an intermediary."[41] You reach out to not just the decision makers, but also to actual people employing your product, such as end users and administrators. Find out what questions they ask when using your product and when trying to solve their problems. You might end up designing solutions that meet their current and future needs.

Customers love listening to each other

A great way to incorporate customer listening is to facilitate ways for customers to listen to each other. Customers adore learning from other customers. They tell me they want to improve from the experience of others, rather than solve things in a vacuum and recreate the wheel. The Walker *CS2020* report indicates, "More companies are beginning to understand the importance and value of initiating ways for customers to network and learn from each other. Customer councils, user communities, discussion forums, and user groups offer opportunities for customers to interact and share best practices with each other; solving problems before they occur. Customers see tremendous value in learning from peers, and it's often difficult for them to organize such encounters on their own."[42] Provide networking opportunities and user communities that give customers the platform to share lessons learned, their approaches, and best practices.

Learning from your customers should be an integral part of your Customer Success and onboarding strategies.[43] So, start listening, build empathy, and understand what your customers want and need. Pick up the phone today to start a conversation. You just might create a customer for life.

WHAT MATTERS

» Empathy and design thinking help you innovate your Customer Success programs and services to best meet the needs of your customers.

» Start by calling a couple customers every week for a short chat and find out what you can learn from them. See what trends are revealed.

READY TO ONBOARD?

» How do you currently listen to customers?

» How can you build empathy and design thinking principles into your Customer Success programs and innovations?

CHAPTER **11**
Driving Customers to Value

After the deal is signed, the real work begins. It's important to engage customers before they start looking elsewhere. Orchestrated Onboarding helps you quickly drive your customers to value, so they stick around, now and later. Value is most relevant during the crucial onboarding period when customers have high expectations of your product and you have limited time to meet their expectations. In this chapter, we'll discuss first value and then explore quick wins and phased deployments to decrease the time it takes customers to be successful in your product.

The trough of disillusionment

In the days when software was sold as a perpetual license, it wasn't compelling for B2B software companies to move customers quickly toward success. After a lengthy sales cycle, companies received a large lump payment and were off looking for the next prospect. During this time, customers were willing to wade through what Gartner calls the "trough of disillusionment" in their extended journey to benefit from their purchases. Gartner's hype cycle for new innovations starts with high expectations, which are quickly followed by deflated interest as the new technology fails to deliver.[44] Eventually, the innovation meets

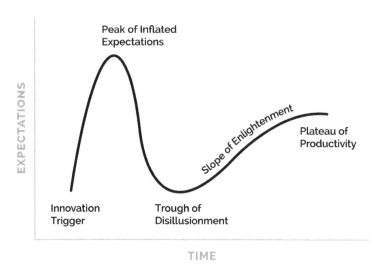

Figure 14: The Gartner Hype Cycle[47]

the needs of the users in the "plateau of productivity." Figure 14 shows the Gartner image.

When you apply the hype cycle to the B2B customer journey, you might see a similar trend—especially when products are sold in the perpetual license model. Customers go through high expectations during the sales cycle and then hit a trough of disillusionment when there's no onboarding, as implementations drag out, and if the product is hard to use. In the *2020 Customer Onboarding Report*, nearly 50 percent of the respondents said it takes from 60 to 90 days to onboard new customers, as shown in Figure 15. That stretch of time creates a huge trough for customers to fall into. Thankfully, according to the subscription analytics company Baremetrics, even though customers don't see immediate value due to delays, the implementation usually gets back on track and then value is eventually realized, as shown in Figure 16.[45]

Onboarding Time

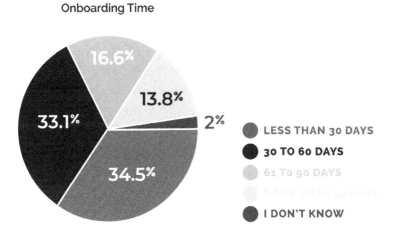

Figure 15: 2020 Customer Onboarding Report: On average, how many days does it take to onboard a new customer?

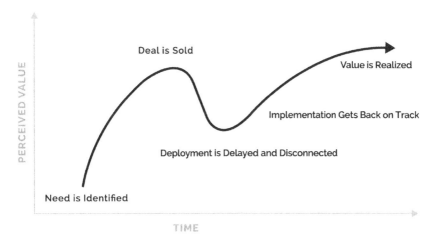

Figure 16: Baremetrics B2B software trough of disillusionment

First value

In today's quick moving world, customers want to see fast results. They are no longer tolerant of the trough of disillusionment. In a subscription economy, you can't afford the delays, frustrations, and long implementations that were acceptable with perpetual licenses. Since accounts invest less initial time and money up front, you don't have their full commitment until you prove value in your product. Just like you have only one chance to make a first impression, you have one chance to guide customers to first value—the moment when customers first realize the benefits of using your product.

Shreesha Ramdas, Senior Vice President at Medallia, Founder at Strikedeck, explains, "The human mind is designed to make conclusions and frame perceptions about a product in a time sensitive manner. Such is the challenge SaaS companies face on a regular basis, to convey product value to customers, before they think of switching to alternative products. The window they have to make this decision is usually quite small, and that is the only time companies have to generate the [time to first value] TTFV."[4746]

When you guide customers to first value, your company benefits by keeping the doors open. Brian Gentile, Board Chairman and CEO Coach, notes that accelerated time to first value helps reduce churn, increase revenue, and improve revenue recognition.[48] First, rapidly demonstrating value to stakeholders and users in the account gets them to stick around for the long term. The increase in renewing accounts, compounded over the long run, adds up to a lot more revenue for you. What makes the subscription model so powerful is that recurring revenue accumulates with each new subscriber. As long as you acquire new accounts faster than you lose them, your revenues grow exponentially.[49] Second, when people quickly adopt and use your product, usage increases at a faster pace. They promptly purchase additional modules and seats to roll out

> *When you guide customers to first value, your company benefits by keeping the doors open.*

across their organization, which is especially valuable when your company has a "land and expand" sales approach. Third, quick value improves revenue recognition. Many companies don't move new sales bookings to recognized revenue until customers achieve initial milestones. In this case, the faster you get to a first deliverable, the better it is for your books.

Rick Nucci, co-founder and CEO of Guru, has observed that many startups fold because of the inability to quickly prove their worth to customers. Nucci says, "One thing I kept hearing from founders of legacy products that had shuttered was some variant of, 'We couldn't justify our existence, so people stopped buying.' The ability to demonstrate value to customers can determine whether a startup generates a wave of sustainable success—or fades into irrelevance with the next tide."[50]

In the world of Customer Success, you often hear folks talk about value. In particular, the term lifetime value (LTV) is thrown around. While LTV is an important metric for subscription offerings, it keeps you beholden on the future. As you know, I'm a fan of what happens at the *beginning* of customer journeys,

> *First value is an essential measure to put on your radar.*

because those first 90 days make or break long-term relationships. That's where Time to First Value (TTFV) comes in. Since we're talking value, let's get clear on meanings:

Value: the importance, worth, or usefulness of something.

Lifetime value (LTV): a prediction of the net profit attributed to the entire future relationship with a customer.

Time to first value (TTFV): the moment when customers first realize the value of your product.

First value is an essential measure to put on your radar. It ensures your customers are on track to reach their goals in your product. The quicker you drive customers to wins by using your product the more customer loyalty, retention, and revenue will grow. Despite this significance, it's pretty rare to find a company that measures first value. In fact, the *2020 Customer Onboarding Report* shows that less than half the companies track how long it takes customers to reach first value in their product, as shown in Figure 17. Rather than joining the crowd that ignores this significant measure, explore what it means for your company and for your customers. Once you're able to measure first value, then investigate ways to decrease the time it takes customers to find your product useful.

Time to First Value

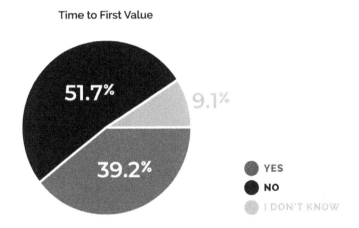

Figure 17: 2020 Customer Onboarding Report - Do you track how long it takes customers to reach first value of your product?

How to determine first value

While you might eventually have a different first value metric for each of your products and for each segment of your customers, start with something simple. Consider milestones and deliverables that quickly demonstrate benefit to customers in one segment or for one product. Some people call this benefit the first 'Aha!' moment users have with your product. As examples, Dropbox's first value is the initial time a customer adds a file to a shared folder, and Facebook defines first value as when a user connects with ten friends in the first week after signup.[51] However, 'Aha' moments are more obvious for consumer products, because users find worth in their experiences so quickly. For B2B software products that take a long time to implement, you'll need to explore how you can quickly drive customers to meaningful insights and deliverables.

It's important to know that first value is *not* about the value you want to deliver. To illustrate, you might determine that first value for your customers is completing their first workflow, or that a percentage of users are active in the system. Those metrics might demonstrate to your company that customers are engaged, stickier, and likely to renew. However, how do you know those activities demonstrate first value to your customers? You don't.

First value is about what resonates for *customers*. That's why, even if you hire me to tell you what first value is at your company, I can't without first learning from your customers. Conversations with customers help you hear the language and metrics they use to justify their investment in your solution. You'll find out the specific objectives that justify the time, effort, and funding they allocate to your system. Explore what's important to customers by asking them:

- How do you know you achieve value with your product?
- Do you have an 'Aha!' moment? If so, what is it and how do you arrive at 'Aha?'
- How long does it take to achieve value, or 'Aha?'
- What are the obstacles that prevent you from reaching first value?
- What tools do you need to reach first value quickly?

How to decrease time to first value

Once you know what's important to customers and how long it takes them to get to first value, explore how to decrease that time. Shreesha Ramdas of Medallia Strikedeck, emphasizes, "The way to create positive experiences around your product is to make your customers reach the Time to First Value at the earliest possible moment. When customers quickly identify the value you deliver, they stick around long enough to have a high lifetime value."[52]

The Orchestrated Onboarding framework is designed to ensure customers reach first value quickly. The following approaches in your onboarding program will help decrease time to first value:

Success plans: Partner with customers to capture their objectives during the buyer journey and in the early stages of onboarding. Specifically, identify and agree on what their first value is in the success plan.

Quick wins: With quick wins, you rapidly guide customers to value with your product, even when the product isn't fully implemented. That way, customers start receiving value immediately. We'll discuss more about quick wins in the next section.

In-app guidance: To help people reach value in your product quickly, consider tools specific for this purpose to guide new users to milestones within your product, like sharing a workflow or creating automated alerts.

Learning pathways: Prescriptive, role-based learning pathways enable users to rapidly learn and adopt your product. While CSMs may step in for human interactions, scalable training resources move customer towards first value at their own pace.

High, low, and tech-touch programs: Provide the right touch at the right time for the right customer segment. Learning pathways and in-app guidance are great tech-touch approaches.

Phased deployments: Long deployments delay first value and bring about the trough of disillusionment that was common with perpetual licenses. We'll discuss phased deployments later in this chapter.

Customer maturity model: Take advantage of the maturity models included in the Expand stage to guide customers through your product or platform in a cohesive way that goes from basic to more complex use cases, and from basic product modules to more advanced ones.

Quick wins

ServiceSource finds when customers don't see results in the first 90 days, their renewal likelihood drops to as low as 10 percent.[53] What happens when your product takes longer than 90 days to set up? We had exactly that challenge at Ace Analytics. Our analytics tool often took six, nine, even 18 months to embed into customers' software. Using quick wins, customers were able to benefit from our product in the first few months, improving the odds of renewal even during long implementations.

What are quick wins? Let's parse the words:

quick: fast in development or occurrence; a rapid succession of events

win: to succeed in arriving at a place or a state

Quick wins are ways to make your product useful to new customers even before your product is fully deployed.

Benefits of quick wins

Quick wins are especially helpful when onboarding and implementations are long or complex. They break things down into achievable nuggets for teams to commemorate along the journey. When customers feel accomplished with your product right away, you're on the road to customer loyalty and success.

Since speed is of utmost importance during onboarding, it's important to rapidly drive customers to value with your product, even when the product isn't fully implemented. Quick wins benefit both customers and the teams supporting them. They deliver immediate satisfaction at the beginning of the customer relationship where it's most needed and most expected. Quick wins help your customers look good and celebrate initial successes with your product, even during the Adopt stage. They also allow the teams on the customer side to show their progress to their internal teams and stakeholders. As a result, customers are grateful they purchased your product, rather than stuck in buyer's remorse and doubt. You gain by keeping customers accountable and staying strategic.

> *Quick wins are ways to make your product useful to new customers even before your product is fully deployed.*

Creating quick wins

When I shared the quick wins concept with a company that provides a digital experience management platform, they announced, "This is great. We'll get customers to log in for our quick win."

Logging into your product is not a quick win. I learned from Customer Success leader Mikael Blaisdell that customers buy software for three reasons: to save money, to make more money, and to align with regulations.[54] So while your product is likely incredible, I doubt customers save or make money just by logging in. Instead, think about their use cases and goals. Reports and dashboards often provide immediate value because the people using your product can make better business decisions. If you can set up an automated workflow and demonstrate the time and money you save your customer, you have a good quick win on your hands.

Quick wins examples

Here are examples that illustrate quick wins.

A software vendor builds workflows for managers of large properties to use for cleaning and renting their properties. Loading property details into the software is time consuming and difficult. Rather than waiting to engage customers until after they load all their properties into the system, I guided them to create a quick win by adding just one property into the system. To facilitate this process, they created quick-start guides and self-paced training. These tools move customers forward without hand-holding from CSMs. Once the first property is loaded, the CSM and customer review it together and determine the next milestone.

Another software vendor that provides a Customer Success platform delivers quick wins by providing two environments for new customers: a basic production environment, as well as a staging environment. Users quickly get to work in the production environment, while at the same time consultants integrate the staging environment with their data sources. When the staging environment is approved, the two environments are merged. This is a great example of providing services that enable customers to easily gain value in your product.

Remember the company who thought logging in was a quick win? We determined that not just reports, but automated alerts generated from the reports, would provide the most benefit. That became their first quick win.

And at Ace Analytics, since the implementation was a long process, we set up prototypes to highlight functionalities most valuable to the customer's project for our first quick wins.

Rather than randomly picking an achievement such as navigating your product, listen to what's important to customers. Find out the milestones and results they want and need in those first few weeks of use. Provide a menu of quick wins that aligns with each customer segment or with unique use cases, deliver several quick wins along the implementation process if it's a long one, and align with milestones at 10, 30, 60, and 90 days.

How to construct quick wins

Start by defining one quick win that aligns with the value your customers need from your product. Then, pilot the quick win with a small group of new customers to find out how it works for them. Once you have a working quick win, create assets and playbooks to make it consistent across all CSMs and customers, and scale the approach. After quick wins are working well, partner with the Customer Education and Support teams to produce self-paced and instructor-led content to guide customers to their quick wins without having CSMs do all the work. Then when you have a solution that has impact, build out a menu of quick wins, leveraging what you learned from the first one.

The Embark and Handoff stages of the Orchestrated Onboarding framework are good times to start discussing quick wins with new accounts. Find out what make sense. Once you agree on the quick win to aim for first, capture it in the success plan. Then, during the Adopt stage, you incorporate the quick win for the customer, even as your full product is being implemented. Consider aligning training—self-paced or instructor led—to guide users to common quick wins. For example, if a quick win is to create a report that drives actionable insights, make sure your content covers *how* to create the reports. An additional service might be a consulting package to customize reports.

Phased deployments

Another way to keep customers from falling into the trough of disillusionment is to stagger deployments. Phased deployments mean chunking the implementation process into achievable components that provide value along the way. Customer Success leader Nello Franco asserts that, "Even if your solution can provide an order of magnitude return on investment, don't try to get there all at once. Provide quick wins for your customers by phasing your deployment." Franco insists that first value should be measured in days or weeks (rather than months), depending on the complexity of the product and your onboarding process.[55] The phased deployment culminates in a smooth customer journey; no trough of disillu-

Phased deployments mean chunking the implementation process into achievable components that provide value along the way.

sionment to fall into here! The image in Figure 18 from Baremetrics[56] shows that phasing the value along the journey generates a smooth and consistent customer journey.

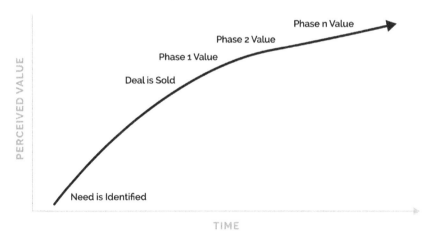

Figure 18: Baremetrics B2B phased approach

I worked with a company whose product is a CRM platform. Their customers are so overwhelmed with all the possible ways to use and customize this platform, they often don't get any value at all. We explored ways to drive their customers to initial value in the CRM system. While the quick wins approach was helpful, the real change came when the company moved away from selling and implementing their infinitely adaptable platform to selling and implementing *distinct products*. Customers now grasp just what they purchased and reach value in weeks rather than months. For this CRM company, focusing on customer value, quick wins, and phased deployments was all encompassing. It changed how they develop, market, sell, and onboard their product.

Bring customer value front and center at your company. Start by learning what first value means for your customers. Then, capture a baseline for how long it takes customers to reach their first goal today. Next, incorporate quick wins and phased deployments in your onboarding program to ensure your customers reach first value quickly and easily.

WHAT MATTERS

» The trough of disillusionment is part of an innovation cycle, identified by Gartner, that starts with high expectations and is quickly followed by deflated interest as expectations are not met.

» First value is the moment when customers initially realize the benefits of using your product.

» The less time it takes customers to reach first value, the better.

» Quick wins are ways to drive customers to value quickly.

» Phased deployments help customers avoid the trough of disillusionment and reach value quickly.

READY TO ONBOARD?

» When you ask customers about their first value, what do they tell you?

» What is time to first value at your organization?

» What are possible quick wins at your company?

» How long are your deployments?

» How can you phase the deployment of your products?

CHAPTER **12**

Measuring the Impact

Customer Success is a new and exciting industry, but not everyone is convinced yet about the value we provide. It's our responsibility to prove the value of our product to customers, and we also must prove the value of our Customer Success services to management. This is both a challenge and an opportunity. Mikael Blaisdell, Executive Director of The Customer Success Association, notes, "The true goal of Customer Success is getting the decision-makers at both the customers and our company to acknowledge and confirm receipt of the tangible value that we deliver. It's about money. That's the proof of value that counts."[57]

No one cares if you don't show results

Blaisdell is concerned because Customer Success professionals often shy away from metrics, data, and financials. My experience aligns with his. When I spoke at a conference about creating go-to-market plans for premium Customer Success services, I asked the Customer Success leaders in the room whether their organizations run as cost, cost recovery, or as profit and loss (P&L) centers. I got back a sea of blank stares. (Don't worry if these are new terms for you— they are defined in Chapter Fourteen.)

The challenge with defining meaningful metrics is that many teams are in the dark when it comes to data. In fact, several respondents in the *2020 Customer Onboarding Report* said they want and need more data. One told me they are desperate to measure results and track progress in an analytical way. In fact, I find it challenging when I work with companies to get them to share relevant baseline metrics so we can measure the impact of working together—they just don't have the data. As a result of the data gap and the need to run Customer Success as a business, Customer Success teams are often sidelined, disregarded, and viewed as an unnecessary expense. Then, when budgets get tight, guess who's first to go?

I fell into this trap myself. Earlier in my career, I led a Customer Education team at a startup. Our customers knew the training offerings were first-rate, and I shared the rave reviews and attendance metrics with my management team. But I didn't connect the impact of our deliverables with the influence on the business bottom line. I didn't know, and therefore couldn't share, that enabled customers are more likely to renew, have higher product usage, and higher customer satisfaction. Unfortunately, this had major consequences. When cost

It's up to you to demonstrate how to decrease churn, reduce internal support costs, shorten the time to first value, and increase customer net retention.

cutting was deemed necessary, my entire team and I were let go because management didn't understand the advantage we delivered to the company overall. Getting laid off was a great lesson in the importance of measuring the worth customer-facing teams provide. Now, I make metrics a priority when I interface with companies.

It's not enough to hope leaders notice all the hours you and your team work to onboard and enable customers. (Remember, hope is not a strategy!) Most likely, management doesn't fully understand what you and your teams do all day, nor the greater impact you have on the business. So, you need to tell them. When you measure and communicate the impact customer onboarding, enablement, adoption, and other Customer Success services have on making customers successful, you're perceived as an investment, not a cost.

Understanding metrics

It's up to you to demonstrate how to decrease churn, reduce internal support costs, shorten the time to first value, and increase customer net retention. Respondents in the *2020 Customer Onboarding Report* share a wide range of measurements to show their impact on Customer Success, as shown in Figure 19. A surprising 10 percent don't measure anything at all. That's a missed opportunity. Understanding metrics helps you have better discussions with your leaders and prove value to both your organization and to your customers.

Onboarding Metrics

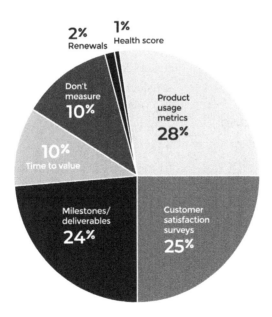

Figure 19: 2020 Customer Onboarding Report – How do you measure
the success of the customer

Metrics come in two flavors: lagging indicators and leading indicators.

Lagging indicators. A lagging indicator is available after a period of time. Lagging indicators are probably what your executives care about most. Leaders want customers to renew and to buy more, however the renew and upsell opportunities may not happen for another 12, 24, or even 48 months. Common lagging indicator metrics include renewal rates, net retention, and total lifetime value. These indicators confirm trends and changes in trends, but aren't helpful for showing immediate impact on your efforts. While a renewal in the bank is the ultimate indicator of Customer Success, you can't wait until the end of the license period to know if your onboarding and enablement programs have impact.

Leading indicators. Leading indicators are immediately observable and allow you to take the pulse of customers along their journey. These measurements can predict lagging indicators like renewals. Leading indicators may include metrics, such as the milestones achieved during onboarding, payment behavior, support tickets logged, product usage, customer satisfaction, and services used. Look at the full list in the customer health score section below, then determine what's most appropriate for your organization to measure. It's critical for you to track the leading indicators to demonstrate how engaged your customers are along their journey. That way, you won't be thrown at renewal time.

...take the pulse of customers along their journey.

Measure your impact

To measure your impact, start by gathering what truly matters to executives and the board. Ask yourself if there is one metric that drives your company. You might hear the metric discussed at company meetings and reported at board meetings. This might be the annual contract value (ACV), annual recurring revenue (ARR), product usage, or lifetime value (LTV). Reducing such internal costs as support tickets might be a focus. Some businesses focus on ACV, others LTV.

Next, explore how your efforts impact that master metric. Dig into existing systems to uncover influence. Don't waste time trying to prove causation or wait a year to show that onboarded customers have higher renewals. Instead, explore leading indicators like product usage, Net Promoter Score (NPS), customer health score, and customer engagement metrics to show correlation between those measurements and your services.

A colleague of mine at a database platform company wanted to understand the effect his customer enablement programs had on customers, so spreadsheet in hand, he manually worked his way through Salesforce account records to compare companies that benefited from his services and those that did not. He uncovered data that showed enabled customers buy *eight* times more software than customers who don't. Companies I assist regularly find customers who are proactively onboarded and trained are 50 to 150 percent more likely to renew. At Ace Analytics, well-trained customers were 20 percent more likely to renew and they had a 15 percent higher Net Promoter Score.

You can easily explore the value you provide to customers, too. The main thing is to keep it simple. Start with straightforward explorations and see what you uncover. Talk to customers, and gather anecdotal evidence in a spreadsheet. While you may not be able to show causation, the data you bring is useful in convincing management to assign resources, such as a data scientist, to dig in deeper.

Start with a baseline

In order to highlight your influence, capture the state of the business before you implement new programs like customer onboarding and enablement. If a baseline doesn't exist, then it's up to you to put one in place. Ask customer-facing teams these simple questions:

- How long does it usually take to onboard new customers?
- What is the level of effort required to onboard customers?
- What are the issues that usually have to be resolved during onboarding?

Once you collect this information from a handful of internal teams, roughly calculate the internal costs to onboard each new account. For example, I worked with a company that provides manufacturing software for complex solutions. Because of their gaps in onboarding and enablement strategy, their customers relied on support agents to provide them what they needed to adopt the product. In this case, calculating the cost of extra support to assist every new account provides you an idea of what the internal outlays were. If an agent makes $100 per hour, the average agent spends ten hours during onboarding resolving issues from new customers, and you bring on 30 new accounts each month, the internal costs come to $360,000 per year.

Next, listen to customers. Explore what onboarding involves from their perspective and ask how satisfied they are with the onboarding experience. Simple questions can easily demonstrate their return on investment (ROI):

- How many hours a week did the onboarding program save you and your team?
- Did the onboarding program help you get more out of the product? If so, can you measure that?
- Are you able to make or save more money while using our product?
- What is the average user's time worth per hour or day?

After you have this data, calculate how many hours they save and how many people use your product. Multiply the hours by their average hourly rate, and you have a number to demonstrate ROI. For example, if the customer saves 30 hours and has 50 users who are paid on average $100 an hour, their ROI from your services would be $150,000.

In addition to a decrease in support costs and an increase in customer ROI, you might include your company's current renewal and upsell rates, churn rates, and average deal size in the baseline metrics. Find out what the current customer satisfaction or Net Promoter Scores are, if they are available. Once you gather baseline metrics, capture a snapshot of the initial numbers, then record the quarterly trends as you implement your programs.

Track your efforts

Another way to prove your team's value is to track the efforts it takes to onboard and enable new customers. When management doesn't see the details, they assume the new approach is unmanaged and they may choose to remove it. Tracking efforts on a spreadsheet is a fine way to start—you don't need to wait for that elaborate Customer Success platform. Record the specific activities you and your team perform to onboard customers. Then measure how your team spends their time. You want to understand how long customer-facing activities take and how many touchpoints customers need to reach quick wins, milestones, and deliverables. This helps you analyze which efforts are working and where to invest the energy of your group. At Ace Analytics, we created a custom object in Salesforce to track Customer Success staff activities. Being a new team, it was important to understand where our efforts were going. We used this data to refine the program and also to validate the transition from a reactive fire-fighting team to a proactive prescriptive workforce with Ace Analytics leaders. Management takes a risk when funding a new approach and they need to see that the investment is worthwhile.

Tracking customer health

You may wonder about the "customer health score" I keep mentioning. Let's define it, since it's an important way to benefit from leading indicators. When done well, the customer health score assesses the current state of accounts, while helping you anticipate whether customers will renew and expand, or churn. This score should include a number of criteria to accurately measure the customer's relationship with your product and your services. Consider including the following touchpoints:

Onboarding milestones and deliverables reached

Support tickets logged
- *Note that while you don't want customers logging excessive support tickets, when customers don't log any tickets at all, that should raise an alarm that they aren't using the product.*

Training courses attended and completed

Services engagements

Product usage

Relationship strength, sentiment score, or other subjective input

Webinars attended

Participation in Voice of the Customer programs

Net Promoter Score

Products purchased

Payment behavior

Some companies implement predictive analytics with an algorithm that conglomerates dozens of criteria. However, many companies consider it a challenge to do math with more than five metrics. Some Customer Success experts declare you should have less than twelve criteria. Customer Success leader Lincoln Murphy stresses that, "Product usage is the moneybag metric."[58] But that depends on your product and your users. The customers of one company with whom I worked use the product only when they perform drug trials, which results in intense waves of living in the product and then not touching it again for months on end. Consider the impact of each possible input and whether it helps customers create value.

Since not all criteria are equally important, explore weighting each criterion to improve the accuracy of the score. For example, onboarding milestones and deliverables might accurately measure customer health more than product usage, or vice versa. Your final metric might be a numerical rating from 1 to 5, traffic signals of red/yellow/green; or a grade of A, B, C, D. It doesn't matter which you choose or where you track your customer health score. Spreadsheets are fine—what's important is that you just start tracking it.

Others don't care about Customer Success and onboarding as much as you and I do. Constantly demonstrate your value to internal teams, management, and customers. There's a common saying, "What gets measured gets managed," so start tracking and measuring what you do. Make it a regular part of your week to measure what matters and then spread the word! People wonder what you and your team are doing, and it helps when you show them. Share your findings with others rather than waiting to be asked. The trends that appear just might help you get more resources.

WHAT MATTERS

» You must prove your company's value to your customers and your team's value to your management.

» Start with spreadsheets and explore how your offerings correlate with the business metrics.

» It's essential to align with the core metrics your company focuses on.

» A customer health score gathers several criteria to assesses the current state of accounts health and gives an indication of their likelihood to renew.

READY TO ONBOARD?

» What are the most important metrics at your company?

» How will you uncover the correlation of your services on the key metrics?

» Where will you capture the baseline metrics and ongoing trends?

» Do you have a customer health score at your company? How do you use it to engage customers?

CHAPTER **13**

How to Scale Customer Onboarding and Enablement

At most companies, CSMs roll up their sleeves to onboard and enable each new account. They show one user (or perhaps a handful of new users) how to log in to the software and then deliver a nice product tour. Unfortunately, this friendly and high-touch overview creates a predicament: You can't scale. In their haste to fully embrace customers, many Customer Success teams assume everything customer related is their responsibility. They forget they're in an orchestra of customer-facing teams, and assume they need to play every instrument for every customer. Meanwhile other customer-facing teams, such as Professional Services, Education Services, and Support, have been around long before Customer Success. The Orchestrated Onboarding framework leverages the expertise that each of these teams brings to deliver a seamless journey for customers.

Why you can't scale

The CSM-as-solo-artist model means that companies are struggling to scale their Customer Success organizations. Zack Urlocker, COO at Zendesk, defines scaling as the ability for a business to grow revenues faster than expenses.[59] Figure 20 shows an important reason for the struggle: CSMs are too often the ones delivering product training. Loading CSMs with training responsibilities leads to adding more CSMs every time your customer base grows. That means margins won't grow, no matter how many new accounts you close. Eventually, your leaders put a stop to hiring new CSMs because it's just too expensive.

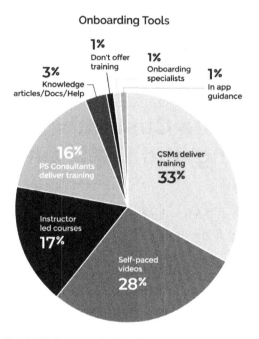

Figure 20: The 2020 Customer Onboarding Report: How do customers learn how to use your product?

Another reason you can't scale when CSMs train customers is that the CSM-as-trainer approach builds ongoing customer reliance on CSMs. One VP of Customer Success told me that while her team of CSMs helps new customers create their first campaign in their marketing product (through individual sessions), customers continue to require assistance from her team beyond that initial training session. As a result, her CSMs spend a great

...scaling is the ability for a business to grow revenues faster than expenses

deal of face time aiding customers with every campaign they build. At a company that delivers an event engagement platform, CSMs guide customers every step of the way for their first "event" in the software. However, because customers don't experience the product for themselves, they reach out to CSMs for the second event they create, for the third one, and so on. When CSMs do the work for their users, the users stay stuck there.

When CSMs do the work for their users, the users stay stuck there.

CSMs at most companies manage more than 20 accounts during the onboarding period alone, as seen in Figure 21. This illustrates there's an urgent need to scale, especially when they are hand holding individual customers and customizing each new customer onboarding. CSMs burn out when they drive product adoption, without having the right skills and tools to be effective. Every time existing accounts add new people, CSMs get pulled into training them, when they should be providing strategic guidance to help the account reach their desired business objectives.

Number of Accounts Onboarded

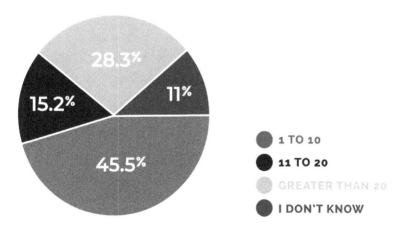

Figure 21: 2020 Customer Onboarding Report - On average, how many accounts does each onboarding person / team manage during the onboarding period?

Scalable customer enablement

No matter how much your customers love them, your CSMs still shouldn't be the ones delivering training. The *2020 Customer Onboarding Report* reveals that most respondents are yearning for courses to lead customers to quick wins. They are desperate for self-paced content to scale onboarding and enablement for both new and existing users. At Ace Analytics, we leveraged courses, documentation, help articles, and other customer enablement offerings to expand the reach of the onboarding program and the CSM team. We plugged the right content for the right users into the right parts of their onboarding and adoption journey through a learning management system and email campaigns. The impact: well-trained customers were more likely to renew and had higher Net Promoter Scores.

Companies that hire me also find a correlation between well-trained customers and higher adoption and renewal rates. At a company that provides software for accountants, the renewal rate for trained customers is 50 percent higher than for untrained customers. At a company that provides process automation software, trained customers are over 150 percent more likely to renew, with 50 to 70 percent higher annual contract values. While this is impressive, both companies suffer from having a small percentage of customers in the well-trained category. This drives home how important it is to scale customer enablement: You have to widen your reach. Single CSMs training an individual, or even small groups of people, to use the product won't impact your business bottom line.

> *No matter how much your customers love them, your CSMs still shouldn't be the ones delivering training.*

When it comes to customer enablement, there's a huge opportunity to profit from the useful approach mastered by the professionals in Customer Education. Customer Education scales Customer Success to onboard and enable your users in four ways: with a one-to many model and with offerings that are repeatable, role-based, and hands-on.

1. **One-to-many model.** While Customer Success is usually a one-to-one, or a one-to-few approach, effective training is designed to be a one-to-many approach. Courses are developed for repeatable delivery, provided by many instructors, and attended by multitudes of customers. Once self-paced courses, or tech-touch, enter the picture, the reach scales exponentially, with little to no cost for each additional person enabled.

2. **Repeatable content.** Instead of having each CSM creating unique classes for individual customers, dedicate resources to design and develop repeatable content that enables customers along their lifecycle. A benefit of this approach is that customers receive a consistent experience, so the success of the learning is not dependent on the particular CSM assigned to them.

3. **Role-based.** Rather than "drinking from a fire hose" to learn the whole product at once, people take the specific courses designed for their unique roles, at the appropriate points in their customer journey. A best practice is to modularize learning and to provide just-in time enablement.

4. **Hands-on.** What most CSMs call training is not actually training. A high-level product overview and demonstration as part of onboarding doesn't provide the effect it should. A more effective approach is to provide hands-on, interactive training that is specific to the work people do in your product. Interactive courses are especially important, because when customers retain what they learn, they no longer lean on CSMs for training.

> *Customer self-sufficiency reduces the load on both Support and CSMs, allowing all teams to manage more accounts as your company grows.*

Customer self-sufficiency reduces the load on both Support and CSMs, allowing all teams to manage more accounts as your company grows. The more specific, interactive, and hands-on the training, the more users retain what they learn, and the less internal teams need to continue supporting customers on basic tasks and "How-to's."

How to build scalable customer enablement content

Rather than waiting until you have a team of curriculum developers and instructors, start scaling with these simple approaches.

1. **Assign a resource.** Instead of directing each CSM do their own thing to enable customers, move content development responsibilities to one or a few team members to build re-usable content. Is there someone on the team that usually jumps in to build content? If so, start with them. There might be a CSM you dedicate to building content for the whole team, or assign as your first Customer Education resource. Take what they build and share it across the team.

2. **Talk to CSMs.** Understand where customers need help, focusing on general use cases that can be used across multiple users.

3. **Talk to Support Agents.** Review the top ten "how-to" cases logged and create simple training modules so customers can help themselves rather than log support tickets.

4. **Talk to customers.** Find out what customers need to learn and how they want to learn it.

5. **Apply the 80/20 rule.** When developing content, apply the Pareto Principle, or the law of the vital few. With a "less is more" approach, produce content to increase customer skills, rather than increase customer knowledge. This means you show users the main routes, or "highways," they need to reach their destination, not every possible side street.

6. **Build a few basic courses.** Pick a role and a use case or two that you gathered from interviewing CSMs and Support agents. Remember to specify what users need to do in your product, not just your product features.

7. **Produce "cheap and cheerful" courses.** I call this the "Target" approach to building courses. Target is a US-based store whose products make you look fashionable without breaking the bank. I encourage you to keep production values simple, especially if your product is constantly changing. Don't spend much time on high production quality unless you know your customers demand it.

8. **Set up a process.** Help Customer Success and Support teams explain where and how to point customers to existing, standardized courses, so they don't have to build and provide the content themselves.

At what stage should you invest in a dedicated Customer Enablement resource? As soon as possible. Customer training and enablement are that important. If customers don't know how to use your software, they won't adopt it, and they won't renew their contracts. Start simple and assign a resource to handle initial course development and delivery. Your education resources can grow as you bring in revenue. When you charge for training, which we'll cover in the next chapter, you can invest the revenue into building the team and developing a robust training offering.

Use your Customer Success teams for what they were hired: strategic, high-value tasks, specific to each customer. Moving CSMs out of ad hoc, repeatable tutoring and coaching keeps them focused on building stellar relationships with their accounts. Building repeatable ways to onboard and enable new and existing customers means you have a greater impact with your onboarding program. Keep it simple and improve as you go. You can't afford to wait.

> **If customers don't know how to use your software, they won't adopt it, and they won't renew their contracts.**

Beware of content jungles

In the "everyone's an author" era, you may think it's marvelous that many teams document what customers need for product adoption. However, just because you and others build content for customers doesn't mean it delivers value. As you build customer onboarding and enablement content make sure you don't create a tangled jungle of content customers have to wade through to find what they need. When many teams have their hands in the enablement pot, it creates customer pain and is costly for your company.[60]

Customer pain

A Customer Success leader from a project management software company told me that, in the name of velocity, everyone builds content at their company. "It's all about getting content out there. Since teams don't want to be blocked, the results are often reactive, and it's hard to get alignment." For tech companies looking to educate users on their products, maximize customer adoption, and minimize churn, the overgrowth of content is a serious problem from the customer perspective. Jungles of content lead to an adoption barrier, an overreliance on people, and customers giving up. I like to negate a famous saying from the film *A Field of Dreams* by saying, "If you build it, they *won't* come." This means that just because you have content "out there" somewhere in the ecosphere, your users will not necessarily find it or use it. Nor will it improve customer onboarding, adoption, and lifetime value just because it exists.

When customers struggle to find what they need to use your product effectively, odds are they won't adopt your product, get value from it, or renew. It's frustrating and time consuming to spend time searching multiple systems only to come up empty handed. In fact, according to McKinsey and IDC, knowledge workers spend on average 19 percent of their working time— about a day a week— just looking for information, not doing productive work. That's staggering for many reasons, not least of which is the math.[61] Let's take a company with 100 employees who each earn an average salary of $80K per year. If they all spend a day a week searching unsuccessfully for information, that's $1.6 million a year in lost productivity, for that company alone.

How can customers gain the skills and knowledge to do their jobs and get value from your product when they are hacking through an overgrown jungle of content? At a supply chain planning software company, the founder was known to spend half days looking for documents in corporate systems to share with new employees, only to come up empty handed. Even more astounding is that even though he wrote those documents himself, he still couldn't find them. Since people could have been doing higher value work, you cost them time and money, which is the opposite of the outcome you want to have.

> *When customers struggle to find what they need to use your product effectively, odds are they won't adopt your product, get value from it, or renew.*

It gets even worse when your content is outdated and uses inconsistent terminology. Customers generally prefer to help themselves. However, as soon as customers are unable to do so, they reach out to your Support and Customer Success organizations, as well as to other "smart humans" in your company that can answer their questions. I worked with a manufacturing software company where customers told me they call each of their contacts within the company until they find someone to take their call and answer their questions. The "smart humans" are often expensive technical experts like product managers and engineers. A customer of a process optimization company shared with me, "The Support team is fabulous, and I use them a lot. In fact, I don't use Support just to deal with what's broken and needs fixing, it's my main learning tool." This customer declared that while they prefer to be self-serving with online content, they head straight to the help desk for all their needs because the content they find is always out of date. While using Support might be awesome from this customer's point of view, it is very expensive from the company's perspective.

Customers want to solve problems themselves. They don't want to stop what they're doing to log yet another support ticket or to call everyone they know. If you don't make it easy and obvious for customers to help themselves, they may just give up and go somewhere else. My colleague Lauren Thibodeau, seasoned Customer Experience and Strategy leader, asked a customer what a company with whom she worked could do better.

Customers want to solve problems themselves.

She heard, "Make it 100 times easier to find information online so I can solve issues myself. I'm pretty resourceful, and usually plow through to figure things out. But my team and I have given up looking. As a result, I'm 100 percent sure we're not using your product to its full benefit."[62]

Company pain

When you build a content jungle, your customers are not the only ones who suffer. Your company undergoes added costs by employing expensive resources to fill the gaps, duplicating content, and employing overlapping tools and systems. When your content doesn't help customers the way they need to be helped, customers reach out to internal experts to solve their problems. In addition, ad hoc issues resolved outside of the Support and Customer Success systems create a loss of valuable information about your product and your customers. You miss out on the big picture and that hurts you in the long term.

While internal teams have the best intention to share what they know with customers, without coordination and communication, it's easy to fall into the bad habit of duplicating efforts and creating similar content in different formats. Take the real-life example of a workflow automation software company that has four completely different "Getting Started" content sets, delivered on four different platforms, developed by four different teams. Even though everyone I talked to at the company wants new customers to get off to a great start, four guides on the same topic result in internal inefficiencies and confused customers. As long as content is created by many authors with ad hoc approaches, you build a jungle of content that quickly becomes stale, out of date, and hard to find—resulting in frustrated customers and overwhelmed employees.

Content strategy best practices

Now that you know the perils of living in a content jungle, let's explore simple best practices to build a scalable content strategy that drives product usage and adoption. While it's great to have many folks across your company creating customer-facing content, most likely it's not built in a coordinated way. All that content requires dedicated resources and processes to guide customers along their journey to success. Best practices include bringing people together, curating content, employing styles and standards, defining user roles and their jobs to be done, and creating learning pathways.

Bring people together. Find all the folks in your organization who create customer-facing enablement content. Most likely they reside on teams of CSMs, Documentation, Support, possibly Professional Services, and even Marketing. If you have a Customer Education or Training department, definitely connect with them as well. The next step is to pull these people together. Consider forming a "content council" with representatives from every group that creates content.

Begin by taking an inventory of customer-facing material. Find out what exists, where it lives, and in which formats. In addition to overlaps and duplications, you will uncover gaps where there's no content.

Remember the company with four Getting Started guides? I found at least ten different platforms where they publish enablement material. They have training modules on a learning management system, "how to" videos on YouTube, knowledge articles on their Support platform, information on the community platform, and on-demand webinars on their website. Does this sound familiar?

Curate content. Rather than building every new enablement approach from scratch, curate from different teams. Curating allows you to quickly drive users to product adoption by leveraging what's already available. Once you know the current state, collaborate with your teammates to determine the content output required for each new release. When you know what needs to be conveyed to customers, then parse out who creates each deliverable and in which format. The priority is to divide and conquer, rather than replicate. This means each team must relinquish ownership of the entire output. To facilitate the cross-functional strategy and processes, you might even appoint a "content czar," "knowledge queen / king," or curator to guide the change. You take all that awesome content and build curated and prescriptive experiences and learning pathways to drive customers toward their goals.

As an example, I've had great experiences when taking self-paced online university classes through Canvas and Coursera. The professors provide recorded lectures and then point to relevant content from across the Internet. Each lesson might include articles on Wikipedia, videos on YouTube, links to pertinent websites, and PDF articles to read. As a learner, I don't care where the information originates--the quality

Rather than building every new enablement approach from scratch, curate from different teams.

of the curriculum and the full experience is what's most important. Many learning management systems allow you to build out courses leveraging content from different sources. When curating, the secret is to make sure each asset remains up-to-date and the links are active.

Create styles and standards. I often talk to teams looking for consistency and standards. Once you have a comprehensive plan to enable customers along their journey, the next step is to develop consistent styles and standards across the content council. This approach keeps customers from getting confused with different terminologies, definitions, and formats in every piece of content they uncover. Style guides help everyone who writes technical content use the same writing approach and the same technical terms. Lauren Thibodeau also encourages teams to define what constitutes "training," compared to other types of valuable content like knowledge base articles and marketing webinars.[63] Lauren and I both suggest you create templates for every output format for content developers to follow, and also define a process and timeline for content updates and maintenance.

Define user roles. Rather than trying to enable all your users on your whole platform, define the unique needs of each user type. When I first joined Ace Analytics, there was just one way for customers to learn. We parked them in a four-day course covering everything for everyone. Professional Services consultants delivered a data dump, and wound up with sore throats after talking at customers for four days. The customers left with plenty of information, but no experience on how to apply it to their jobs. They didn't actually know what to do with the product. The first thing I did was to define the unique roles that used the Ace Analytics product: business analysts, administrators, and developers. Next, I learned what each role needed to do with the product and created specific enablement material for each of them.

...define the unique needs of each user type

Talk with internal teams and customers to map out the different types of roles working with your products. While you might gather a long list of different job titles, explore where these user types overlap to narrow your list to just a handful of roles. At a manufacturing software company, we brought together a group of subject matter experts to brainstorm the different roles of people who work with their product. Very quickly we tallied 51 different roles! Next, we discussed, argued, challenged, and negotiated to narrow the list to seven unique jobs. Using this information, we designed meaningful content and learning pathways for each role.

Consider whether your company has different tiers of users. For example, in the increasingly common business-to-business-to-business (B2B2B) and business-to-business-to-consumer (B2B2C) models, different roles have vastly different needs. Uber and Lyft are familiar examples. These companies need to onboard and enable their drivers first, and then have a separate strategy for enabling the passengers who are the consumers. For the B2B2B example, consider the company that provides a platform to help companies build teams of technical developers from anyplace in the world. Their first layer is B2B: the companies building the team. But then there's another layer: the developers delivering the technical work, who are hired as freelancers. Both the business customers and the freelancers need to be onboarded and enabled on the platform in order for everyone to be successful.

Describe jobs to be done. Once you define your user roles, the next step is to understand the jobs each role "hires" your product to do. A common mistake when enabling users is to focus on your software. I see this instinct at most companies; it's only natural you want to explain how to navigate around your gorgeous user interface and point out all the cool features and things users can do. However, according to Customer Education leader Adam Avramescu, customers don't care about your product.[64] While you and your teams might be enthused about the latest features and functionalities, users just want to be better at their jobs. Providing a tour around your interface is just the surface of customer enablement. Your job is to make them heroes at their companies—not master button clickers in your software.

Build learning pathways. Next, show users the progression of content in context of a visual, role-based learning path, easily accessible on your website. The progression might first guide customers to the quick wins and deliverables you determined together in the success plan. Once the basics are covered, lead them to more advanced use cases in your product. Remember to curate content to create this cohesive and prescriptive guidance for customers and then make sure all customer-facing teams direct customers towards the prescriptive pathways.

The maintenance challenge

As you create content to enable customers, take care your customers aren't wading through a jungle of outdated material. While there's usually an eagerness to write that first course or article, it seems everyone is suddenly swamped with other priorities when it comes to updating content to the latest release. For instance, when I first started at Ace, I pulled together subject matter experts across the company to quickly write and publish the first version of our customer enablement content. People were eager to help and to receive recognition from the CEO on this important project. However, when I asked folks to update what they created for the next release, I heard crickets.

Many teams struggle to stay current because there's the constant chase of the next release. A colleague of mine likens creating new content and new courses to birthing babies. Once a course is created, it's like an infant that forever needs their diapers changed, because there's always the next release to consider. Since customers need current, relevant, and accessible content, make sure you build a maintenance plan into your content strategy.

To solve this challenge, update content and courses for major releases rather than for every minor release. It's also important to band with the product marketing teams to understand the major upcoming changes in your products and address the needs of users when the changes roll out. Rather than revising each course that references every part of your product, build delta training modules which focus on unique changes. Another solution is to modularize your content, so everything is easy to update. That way you simply replace or update specific components rather than redo monolithic courses.

Using technology to scale

Many teams stuck in ad hoc Hell expect new technology to put out their fires and make their lives easier, but it usually only makes things worse. Applying new software systems on top of ineffective or nonexistent processes only creates more jungles to wade through. The *2020 Customer Onboarding Report* shows that spreadsheets and CRMs are most commonly used to scale customer onboarding, as seen in Figure 22.

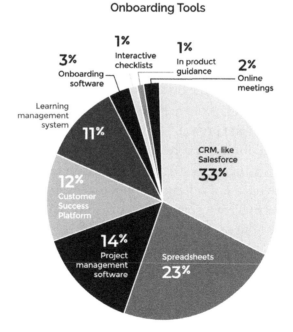

Figure 22: 2020 Customer Onboarding Report - What tools do you use to manage and deliver onboarding?

Many companies with whom I touch base put automated onboarding on their technology wish list. With tools like learning management systems, marketing automation, and Customer Success platforms, you can make this a reality. First, define the prescriptive approach you want new accounts, and also the people using your product in those accounts, to follow in your platform. When you have the content in place, whether it's custom built or curated, plug that into the journey to help people perform their jobs with your platform.

A technology stack optimized to scale customer onboarding and enablement permits you to build high, low, and tech touch approaches, allowing you to scale quickly. To illustrate, I worked with a content security platform company that built an onboarding email campaign with training videos. The emails branch—depending on what users accomplish, or not, in their product. They found that those customers that read more emails and watched the prescribed videos would dive into the product further and file 10 percent less support tickets. The tickets they do file ask more complex questions because they already know the basics. In addition to delivering bite sized tips and tricks through email, the company also offers one-to-one training to dive into the specifics *after* customers have the basics covered through a tech touch.

Onboarding tools. While spreadsheets are popular, don't get stuck there. I worked with a supply chain management company that has a jungle of spreadsheets designed to guide internal teams along every step of the journey. Unfortunately, the processes aren't followed because they are embedded in a spreadsheet that's been filed away in a location that's hard to find. At the appropriate time, invest in the right technology to improve both your internal flow and transparency with customers. Technology solutions for onboarding includes online project management tools, as well as onboarding-specific software. Many of these tools integrate with your CRM. Customer Success platforms allow you to build out playbooks to manage onboarding workflows. When you use marketing automation tools, you build out digital and automated journeys for customers—similar to those like you have for prospects.

Enablement tools. One of the most wished-for tools in the *2020 Customer Onboarding Report* is in-product guidance. Software built for this allows you to show your users how to complete specific tasks right in the product. A learning management system (LMS), another highly requested tool, is what's needed to implement content strategy best practices and deliver customer enablement at scale. Most learning management systems allow you to deliver learning experiences with curated content and learning pathways for each audience. Your team might also benefit from single sourcing tools to scale content development, content management systems to track and maintain all the content you built, and universal search technology to make it easy for you and your customers to find what's needed. You can deliver remote instructor led classes with tools like Zoom, and GotoTraining. For hands-on labs, I recommend remote training environments vendors.

Beware the technology jungle

Just as you need to watch out for a tangle of content, beware of building a technology jungle. While it's natural in the early days when your company is growing fast to secure the tools you need in the moment to get the job done, over time you create a wilderness of overlapping tools and systems. The technology jungle creates internal inefficiencies, as well as higher-than-necessary IT bills. I see companies with numerous learning management systems, multiple video creation and editing platforms, several survey and feedback tools, and dozens of content creation tools. This is not because the needs of each internal team are vastly different, but because they don't coordinate their tool selection efforts. You know things are bad when no one knows how many systems are in place. I worked with a company that had at least seven learning management systems! This tangle of systems requires integrations, customizations, updates, administrators, and complex extract-transform-load processes in order to stitch together data across disparate systems.

The route to building your technology stack is to make sure each system works together and aligns with your goals to scale, orchestrate, build efficiencies, and deliver the impact you need. As with your content review, pull together customer-facing teams to take an inventory of all the tools and systems used by each team and even each team member—to onboard and enable customers. Document all the tools in play, explore where there are overlaps, uncover gaps, and see what's obsolete and needs updating. This is also a great opportunity to identify all the monthly and yearly subscriptions you spend on SaaS tools, because they add up. I know teams who construct consolidation plans and then negotiate for new resources to create scalable customer enablement content based on how much money they save each month and year.

When designing your technology stack, it's also necessary to consider the roles you need in place to administer the tools and systems. Most companies have sales and marketing operations roles to manage the important technology used to drive prospects through the sales funnel. Many businesses are adding a Customer Success operations role, rather than expanding the role of CSMs to manage all the tools and the technology stack. Having the right people in this role will enable your ability to scale, too.

While an untamed jungle is an essential component of a biodiverse world, it's a hostile environment when customers can't navigate through your content to get what they need. Building a glorious garden with shrubs, flowers, lighting, signage, and pathways makes life better for both you and your customers. To translate into the language of customer onboarding and enablement, help customers adopt your product with cross-functional collaboration, content curation, a job-role focus, consistent styles and standards, and a cohesive technology stack. Scaling customer onboarding and enablement is critical to both you and your customers' success.

---- ----

WHAT MATTERS

» Scaling is the ability for a business to grow revenues faster than expenses.

» Too often, companies are unable to scale because CSMs are attempting to onboard and enable each new customer.

» Customer Education is the solution to scaling Customer Success and onboarding with a one-to many model, and with offerings that are repeatable, role-based, and hands-on.

» In the "everyone's an author" era, it's easy to build content jungles that make it hard for customers to learn.

---- ----

READY TO ONBOARD?

» Bring teams together into a content council to curate content.

» Manage your technology stack to avoid duplication and added expenses.

» How many people and teams across your organization create customer enablement content?

» In how many different formats is customer enablement delivered?

» How many different tools and systems are used internally to build, store, deliver, and track enablement content?

CHAPTER 14

Premium Packages

Premium Customer Success packages are the next best practice to explore on your onboarding journey. I've told you of the importance of onboarding. You may be surprised that I'm now telling you to charge customers for it. Why is that? Because Orchestrated Onboarding benefits both you and the customer. You can charge for onboarding services, of course, once you've listened to customers and implemented an Orchestrated Onboarding framework that drives them to the outcomes they want.

Creating and selling premium Customer Success packages may be your gateway to making you and your customers more successful. Take a look at these benefits:

- Customers are accountable and engaged.
- Customers are satisfied and loyal, with higher customer satisfaction.
- Renewal rates are higher.
- Your offerings differentiate you from the competition.
- CSMs are more strategic as they move away from reactive repeatable tasks.
- You scale your Customer Success organization more easily.

- You hire the resources your team needs to meet the growing demands of customers.

- Sales reps understand the value of Customer Success and are excited to partner with you and your team.

While many of these benefits seem too good to be true, charging for premium services has a positive impact for both you and your customers. That's why it's time to take customer-facing services as seriously as you take the software products. Gainsight, a Customer Success platform vendor, summed it up well: In SaaS, where product is developed and distributed as a service, services are developed and packaged as a product.[65] You turn services into desirable products that customers want to purchase, and then charge for them. As with any product you bring to market, your customer onboarding and enablement programs need to be branded, marketed, and sold as bona fide products in your company.

Creating and selling premium Customer Success packages may be your gateway to making you and your customers more successful.

There's a cost to being a cost center

Before Customer Success became common place, companies usually ran services organizations as profit and loss businesses with high margins. Now that the focus is on the ultimate indicator, customer renewals, many companies offer customer onboarding, enablement, and CSM services to customers at no costs. The 2020 Customer Onboarding Report confirms this showing that 70 percent of companies do not charge for onboarding services, as shown in Figure 23. As a result, all these companies and their customers miss the benefits of premium Customer Success

...it's time to take customer-facing services as seriously as you take the software products

packages. While charging customers continues to be a hot topic for debate in the Customer Success community, a complimentary offering does not mean it's free to build, deliver, and maintain. Even in Customer Success there's no such thing as a "free-lunch."

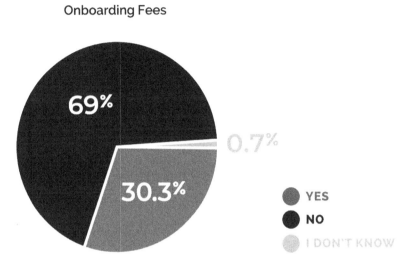

Onboarding Fees

69%

0.7%

30.3%

● YES
● NO
● I DON'T KNOW

Figure 23: 2020 Customer Onboarding Report - Do you charge for customer onboarding?

The challenge with giving away valuable Customer Success services is that your team will be regarded as a cost center—even when your efforts increase customer retention. Your company suffers when Customer Success is free:

- You get by on limited resources, even when other teams are hiring.

- You are unable to deliver the best-in-class services customers need to reach their outcomes.

- You stay stuck in fire-fighting mode, rather than moving ahead of the curve with proactive and prescriptive programs.

- You battle to get customers to show up for onboarding, implementation, and enablement meetings.

- CSMs chase down existing customers while juggling a wave of new customers.

- Customer retention and support costs increase.

- Ultimately, you and your team are at risk of being cut.

There's a cost on the customer side as well. Of course, customers say they want to pay as little as possible for your product and your services. However, when they don't remunerate you for your valuable services, they aren't accountable. They don't turn up for scheduled meetings, they don't move forward on their parts of implementation plans, their product adoption is low, and they don't get much value from your product. All this leaves you vulnerable because they are more likely to churn.

To charge or not to charge: That is the question.

Despite the assumption that customers don't want to pay, research by PWC finds that customers are willing to pay for good customer experiences. In fact, 86 percent of buyers are willing to spend more for a great customer experience, and the more expensive the item, the more they're willing to pay.[66] It seems customers are more committed to reaching the agreed upon milestones and deliverables when they pay for your services. They are also more likely to work with you—not against you—on the journey.

> *86 percent of buyers are willing to spend more for a great customer experience...*

You likely experience this yourself when you sign up for a free online class. Even with your best intentions, you usually don't start the class—let alone complete it—with everything else on your to-do list taking priority. However, when you pay for learning experiences, you show up, you make time on your calendar to work through the modules, you pass the quizzes, and you make changes in your life as a result of what you learn. That's how your customers behave when they spend money on Customer Success services.

When customers hand over their valuable funds, they have more skin in the game. Companies that charge for onboarding regularly tell me that their customers are more accountable, and that those customers even appreciate being held responsible for their side of things. Customers show up for meetings, partner during the implementation, complete their required tasks, attend classes, and retain what they learn—when they pay for Customer Success services. A process automation company with which I worked finds customers actually use the product *more* when they pay for onboarding.

Across the industry there are heated debates about whether to charge for Customer Success services. Some argue Customer Success should be free since it's in your best interest to enable customers. Others insist customers pay a premium to cover costs and to invest in providing superior services. After several rounds of arguments on each side, the Ace Analytics teams resolved to bundle the best practices customers wanted and needed into premium Customer Success offerings. The revenue generated from Customer Success services provided Ace with the funds to build best-in-class programs, which were used to differentiate the company from others in the crowded analytics software space.

> *Companies that charge for onboarding regularly tell me that their customers are more accountable...*

The premium packages at Ace Analytics included a dedicated CSM, time with a Customer Success Engineer, a subscription to the self-paced learning library, and appropriate Professional Services consulting packages. To ensure the success of these new offerings, we created a go-to-market plan and sought the help of a local advertising firm to design a brand we could proudly promote. On a financial level, we prioritized the success of Ace Analytics customers over high margins and large services profits. We added an uplift to the license price for the Customer Success services, which meant every time the software license renewed, the Customer Success package renewed as well. This allowed teams to partner with customers to maximize their value with Ace long after they were onboarded.

Finance is your new best friend

Charging for Customer Success services may be new for you, so, befriend your finance team. I learned to reach out and connect with my finance colleagues from Jesse Finn, a former Customer Education leader. As a Customer Success professional, you might shy away from connecting with folks who live in the world of spreadsheets and numbers. However, it makes a valuable difference to have finance experts on your side as you bring products to market. A side benefit of my doing this was that I developed long lasting friendships with my finance associates.

Once you decide to charge for onboarding and enablement services, work with the finance teams to determine the best pricing model for your company. Of course, services revenue is usually a drop in the bucket compared to software revenue. While income is important, a large margin seems out of line with the mission of enabling successful customers with your product. Your finance partner should see this revenue as a method of paying for the effort of building and delivering proactive premium packages. Your priority is still to demonstrate the impact your offerings provide on customer engagement, retention, and loyalty. Next, make sure Finance allocates the income from your new products back to your team. Otherwise, you'll be challenged to invest and grow your team and to improve your offerings.

As you work jointly with your finance partner, it's helpful to understand some of the terms they use. Take a look at the glossary to learn the difference between bookings and revenue margins, and more.

Pricing models

Before you consider pricing strategies for your premium Customer Success packages, it's important to know whether your organization operates as a cost, break-even, or profit center. See the definitions below to learn more.

Cost Center: A cost center is a department within a company that does not directly add to the profit of a company. While cost centers contribute to a company's profitability indirectly, they add operating costs to the business bottom line. Margins are negative in a cost center.

Cost Recovery Center: Also known as a "break-even" center, this is a department within a company with the intention of having a zero profit. So, rather than being a cost to a company the goal is to invest all profits back into the department, to keep the organization growing.

Profit and Loss Center: A profit and loss center (P&L) is a department within a company that contributes to profitability directly through its actions. It is treated virtually as a separate, standalone business, responsible for generating revenues and earnings. The profit and losses are calculated separately on accounting balance sheets, with a goal to have positive margins.

Ask your finance partners the best approach for your product and team, both for the short term, and for the longer term. Then engage the folks in Finance to determine pricing. It's helpful to know industry standards and understand how your competitors charge in order to refine your pricing approaches.

Consider these pricing options:

Required versus optional: When you go with the required option, all license contracts must include Customer Success services. Otherwise, the customer has the option to choose to purchase the services or not.

Separate line item versus bundled with license: Explore whether packages are sold as separate line items on the order, whether they're required or optional—or are they included in the license fees?

Uplift license price versus percentage on top of license: When you bundle premium packages into the license fee, this could be a set amount for all customers or for each customer segment, or a specific percentage on top of the cost of the license (which would generate higher revenues from bigger customers).

One-time fee versus renewing subscription: Will Customer Success services be sold as a one-time onboarding and implementation fee, or will services renew every year with the license renewal? I like renewing packages to keep customers engaged throughout their lifecycle.

Discounts: When you define pricing, that's the time to define discounting policies and how you will reinforce them. Otherwise, you might find your new premium offerings being given away as part of a sales deal, with the value eroding as a result.

There's a trend for software companies to charge a one-time implementation fee for onboarding and consulting services. While this is moving in the right direction, I encourage you to go beyond this and create an ongoing subscription fee that covers the initial onboarding and enablement, as well as high-touch services like a dedicated CSM to help customers maximize their value in your product. Read on to see what would be included in these premium subscription services.

What's in a premium Customer Success package?

Remember that hope is not a strategy. Rather than hoping customers buy the services they need to be successful, package together everything they need to quickly and easily reach their goals. Then charge for the premium package. The Technology Services Industry Association (TSIA) calls this the "complete offer," because selling software to customers is no longer enough for customers to be successful. As a result, TSIA encourages companies to include the services customers need, not as an add-on, but as part of the package.[67]

Investing in building, delivering, and selling premium services packages makes sense as long as you have robust offerings that drive real outcomes for customers. Charging customers to have a call with a CSM once a quarter where they hear, "How's it going?" is not a premium offering. Telling customers to "Call me when you have a problem," doesn't provide much value either. In order to build a meaningful services product, you need to include clear deliverables and outcomes for the offering. Since customers are already used to purchasing support and maintenance, they'll pay for programs that drive positive outcomes.

The Vice President of Consumer Support and Customer Success Operations at a security software company told me they stepped away from the "body shop" business when they defined and delivered a methodology of best practices. Rather than selling "fix-it" services, they now package, sell, and deliver proactive offerings that renew every year. They compare their new offerings to "Value Meals" with the right services included to drive adoption. Onboarding and implementation services are included the first year, then performance tuning and health checks are provided the following years. Customer Success services and training are included throughout the customer journey and at different levels, depending on the package tier purchased.

At Ace Analytics, we bundled offerings from Customer Success, Customer Education, Support, and Consulting services to make it easy for customers to implement, learn, adopt, and excel with the Ace

Analytics product. We bundled the fees into the license sale so that every year when the license renewed, the services package renewed too. We built a high-touch offering for enterprise companies which included unlimited seats in the online learning portal, consulting packages, and a number of hours with a Customer Success Engineer (CSE) to guide technical planning during implementation. Enterprise customers also had regular access to their assigned CSM, who focused on strategic guidance. Mid-size companies received a lower touch approach that included a smaller consulting package, one seat in the self-paced training library, and an assigned CSM. We capped the number of hours available for this group of CSMs, since they handled more accounts than their enterprise counterparts. Finally, small companies received a single training subscription and self-paced guidance in their Customer Success package. Supplemental training, consulting, and CSM hours were available for purchase at an additional fee.

Here's an example for how to package customer-facing services.

Example premium Customer Success packages

Year One

- Implementation services, including customizations, migrations, and integrations

- Dedicated or high touch CSM

- Some level of Customer Success Engineer/Architect

- User enablement/training

- Change management services

- Premium support that includes easy access to a support agent through phone or chat, and a defined turn-around time for issues logged

Year Two and Beyond

- Proactive offerings to increase customer maturity and maximize value

- Ongoing enablement for new users, new products, new product features, and new organizations

- Dedicated or high touch CSM

- Some level of Customer Success Engineer/Architect

- Health checks, performance tuning services

- Premium Support

When does it make sense to produce premium packages? The timing depends on when you have enough proactive components compiled in an attractive package that delivers high value. Then your customers are more willing to pay for it. The recurring revenue you obtain from renewable services subscriptions helps the leaders at your company to sit up and pay attention to what you and your team are doing as well as the impact you have with customers and the bottom line.

Prototype and test

As you design and build new premium packages, make sure to put the design thinking principles covered in Chapter Ten to use. Empathize with your customers to find out what services would make a difference. Learn from internal teams to uncover gaps and avoid duplicating efforts. Once you determine the components of the premium package, build a minimally viable product (MVP) for a single customer segment. Next, pilot this with a handful of customers to get their feedback. Stay agile and iterative during the building process and keep improving as you go. Once the offering runs smoothly and effectively drives the customer behavior you want, tailor the components to address different customer segments and different products. For example, you might have a high-touch enterprise offering that gets good traction. Take that offering, learn from customers in the mid-sized companies, and scale the package down to meet their needs. Once you get that offering working correctly then you can build a self-paced or tech touch set of offerings for small companies.

Take your Customer Success product to market

When you have the makings of a premium services package that drives real outcomes for your customers, put on your product manager hat to define a way to market, sell, and deliver your new offering in a go-to-market plan. At Ace, we didn't take the, "If we build it, they will come," approach. We didn't present a long list of services options to sales reps and customers, hoping they would pick the right one. Instead, we packaged what customers needed to be heroes with our products, priced it properly, and defined how to market and sell the new offering to both sales reps and to customers.

The success of your premium packages is the result of a comprehensive **go-to-market plan**. A go-to-market plan defines the internal and external resources needed to deliver your unique value proposition to customers, achieve a competitive advantage, and enhance the overall customer experience.[68] The go-to-market plan takes factors in the quality of the product and the pricing. I also like to include strategies to sell and market the offering to internal teams like Sales, Customer Success, and Marketing, as they all need to be on board to make the premium offering worthwhile. Since the go-to-market plan improves product definition and communication with internal teams it also keeps you from working in a silo.

How to build a go-to-market plan

The go-to-market plan answers the who, what, why, and how of your offerings. To build your plan, create a document that answers these statements:

- **Who:** Defines the audience, including the internal and external stakeholders to engage.
- **What:** Defines the exact offerings you bring to market.

- **Why:** Explains the purpose and impact your product has on your audience and on your company.

- **How:** Details how to price, sell, market, and deliver your product.

Download go-to-market templates at **OrchestratedOnboarding. com**.

Go-to-market plan template

Executive Summary

What is the high-level overview of your offering and how will you take it to market?

Purpose

What is the offering and why do users need it? The purpose might include a shorter time to first value for customers, reducing the support queue, or increasing product usage. When your program defines outcomes and deliverables and not just the services delivered, then you have a product that customers want to purchase.

Audience

Who is the audience for this product? This might include enterprise companies, small to mid-sized companies, or all customers and partners.

Delivery

How will this product be delivered? Who will deliver it? Delivery options might include onsite consulting, self-paced courses, or a defined set of hours with Customer Success Engineers or Customer Success Managers.

Pricing Strategies

What will you charge for this product? Consider the following pricing options:

- Required versus optional
- Bundled with the license versus separate line item
- Uplift license price versus percentage on top of license
- One-time fee versus renewing subscription

Resources and Costs

- How will you resource this plan?
- What team members, tools, and infrastructure requirements are required?
- How much will it cost to implement the resources?
- What are the delivery costs?
- How does this figure into the business model and the pricing?

Marketing Strategies

How will you market this new offering to internal teams and customers?

- **Internal strategies:** How will you market your offerings internally—to CSMs, Support, and Sales Reps? For example, you might join sales calls, send out monthly internal newsletters, or share wins across the organization.

- **External strategies:** How will you market your offerings externally—to customers and partners? Create collateral to educate existing customers and prospects of your offering, which might include data sheets, press releases, webinars, special offers, and customer-facing FAQs. You could partner with Engineering to provide an in-application banner when your software starts to point users to onboarding and enablement resources.

Sales Plan

How will you sell this product? You'll need both internal and customer-facing plans to sell your new offering.

- Internal strategies: How will you align with sales incentives, including quota, commissions, and club? Include details on how to sell your product in sales enablement programs. Partner with sales management to include your products and selling strategies in sales playbooks and provide incentives to reps for selling your offerings.

- External strategies: What is your plan for selling to new and existing customers? Existing customers could provide a large opportunity for revenue. How can you align with the sales cycle and with other services products to provide a solution sale?

Success Metrics

Which metrics will you use to measure your impact? How will you capture, track, and share the metrics? Make sure what you measure ties into the purpose. For example, if reducing the support queue is the purpose of the offering, then demonstrate the impact on the support queue over time. Measure against business metrics, rather than focus on the services metrics only. Before you launch your new offering, take a snapshot of baseline metrics to compare the impact over time. Consider both the following leading and lagging indicators:

Leading indicators
- Number of customers onboarded
- Time to first value
- Onboarding timeline
- Attach rate of premium packages
- Bookings and margins
- Volume of support tickets and time to close
- Customer health score
- Net Promoter Score

Lagging Indicators
- Renewal rates
- Upsell amounts
- Lifetime value

How to get customers on board even before you onboard them

Ideally, your premium packages will set you apart from the competition. Work closely with your marketing teams to create branding that highlights and sells the value, then design a plan to get customers on board even before you onboard them. Adding slides to the usual sales decks about your onboarding and Customer Success programs to not just highlight the benefits of your offerings but also provide value to companies even before you close the deal.

> *Ideally, your premium packages will set you apart from the competition.*

Next comes the challenging part: Aligning the sales teams. It's essential for sales leaders and their teams to understand what happens after the sales cycle and why they care. They need to grasp the impact your program has on the success of customers, the company, and, especially, what's in it for them. Consider building internal collateral to help them articulate the offering, then go over the details during sales enablement training, sales calls, and sales kickoffs. I'm a big fan of the "drip feed approach" to gently bring new concepts into the consciousness of sales reps with repetition over time. It seems people need to see something around nine times before the message even starts to sink in, so don't think one big announcement at the next sales kickoff is going to do the trick.

Sales enablement slides

Following is an example of slides to include in sales enablement training:

What is the Ace Analytics Customer Success and Onboarding program?

- A program of best practices to guide customers to use Ace Analytics's platform successfully.

Why Ace Analytics Customer Success?

- Our goal is to not just sell our products, but to have customers quickly and successfully implement them, to renew, to buy more, and to be our champions
  - Engaged customers use more product features and buy more
  - Customer Success differentiates Ace Analytics from our competitors
  - CSMs help account managers uncover new opportunities

How Does the Customer Success Program Work?

- CSMs guide customers along an Orchestrated Onboarding journey of best practices to lead customers to success

- Accounts are assigned a Customer Success Manager as their strategic advisor to identify the customer desired business outcomes and to measure the impact

What Customer Success is NOT

- Support 2.0
- Account Management
- The full responsibility of CSMs

Customer Success is everyone's responsibility

- Working together we have a greater chance of success

Orchestrated Onboarding Framework

- We front load the relationship with a prescriptive onboarding program to lead customers to success

- Embark | Handoff | Kickoff | Adopt | Review | Expand

Customer-facing slides

Here's an example of slides to include in customer-facing decks.

What is the Ace Analytics Customer Success and Onboarding program?

- A program of best practices to guide customers through Ace Analytics's platform journey successfully.

- Our goal is to not just have you buy our software, but to quickly and successfully implement it to become a hero within your organization.

- Provide an overview of the Customer Success and onboarding programs

Orchestrated Onboarding

- We front load the relationship with a prescriptive onboarding program to lead customers to success

- Embark | Handoff | Kickoff | Adopt | Review | Expand

Of course, creating a premium services product and a thorough go-to-market plan does not transform your business overnight. My colleague who made this transformation told me that it took about six months to shift their teams away from delivering reactive programs and towards the premium proactive programs. The teams at this security software company worked hard to create simple programs that sales reps could sell, and that customers could easily purchase. Then they assembled a comprehensive go-to-market plan to bring the new offerings to market. They defined incentives for sales reps that had impact. My colleague emphasized how much communication was needed to direct internal teams and sales reps to sell and deliver the new premium packages, and to guide customers to the new approach. So far, the results have been impressive. Sales reps are on board and happily selling the new packages. Escalations are down, NPS scores are up ten points, and customers are excited about the new approach.

With a well-thought-out premium services product and a robust go-to-market plan, you not only build your offerings, you can properly price, market, and sell them. Thinking like a product owner drives engaged internal teams and successful customers. Sales reps are happy because they sell larger subscription deals. CSMs are relieved to not be responsible for doing it all. Customers are delighted to quickly receive ROI on their investment. Management is thrilled because NPS and renewal rates keep increasing. You end up with engaged and enabled companies that are more likely to renew and buy more—as well as scalable Customer Success teams and reduced support queues.

WHAT MATTERS

» Building and selling premium Customer Success packages provide many internal and external benefits to guide you and your customers to success.

» The go-to-market plan answers the who, what, why, and how of your offerings.

READY TO ONBOARD?

» Collaborate with your finance team to define your business and pricing models.

» Consider selling premium Customer Success services as renewing subscriptions that help your customers maximize value year over year.

» Use design thinking principles to design and prototype solutions that best fit your customers.

» Build a go-to-market plan to bring your new product to market successfully.

» List the services you can bundle together to create a premium package at your company.

» Define the outcomes and deliverables the services provide to customers.

» Use the go-to-market plan template to start your go to market plan.

» With whom will your team build a robust go-to-market plan?

- Finance	- Professional Services
- Education Services	- Support
- Customer Success	- Marketing
- Executive team	- All of the above

CHAPTER 15
Putting Orchestrated Onboarding into Practice

Now that you have a grasp of the Orchestrated Onboarding framework, each of the six stages, and the principles, how do you put that into practice at your company? In this chapter, I'll share best practices for you to adopt as you implement Orchestrated Onboarding. I also include examples from many of the companies with whom I've worked. To put the Orchestrated Onboarding framework into practice, learn how to communicate clearly, tailor the framework, and use change management efforts to optimize onboarding at your company.

Customers are overwhelmed

I do business with companies that sell complex software. To be successful, their customers have to migrate data, connect application programming interfaces (APIs), develop customizations, and learn new processes and technologies. These tasks can be formidable for customers—especially when they aren't tech savvy. New users are likely overwhelmed in the early days of purchasing a new solution and all that it entails for their business.

When you throw long task lists and complicated requirements at new customers, they can't process the information. Communications Designer Dr. Echo Rivera indicates it's easy to send customers into cognitive overload during onboarding, since "Our working memory is that space where we're processing, thinking, and trying to fit that new bit of info into its new 'home' in our brains. It's really easy for us to get overwhelmed during this process—especially if there are distractions, we're tired, or we get confused."[69] As you create customer-facing assets, make sure people can easily process what you convey. Otherwise, your new customers will stay stuck in overwhelm, and your onboarding process will get bogged down.

Visuals are magic

In Chapter One, we discussed how brain science comes into play during customer onboarding. It's important to address how people deal with first impressions, confirmation bias, and buyers' remorse, in order to build trusting relationships with new customers. It turns out that neuroscience is also involved with how you communicate the important information you share with customers during each stage of onboarding. That's because our brains process visual information more quickly and more easily than text.

Communicate with visuals

If you want to retain your customers, you need to understand how they learn and retain the details you share with them. That's where visuals come in. I'm sure you know the phrase, "A picture is worth a thousand words." It's due to the fact that the human brain processes visuals up to 60,000 times faster than text.[70] Research shows that people pay attention, understand what you tell them, and use that information more effectively when you show them images.[71]

I learned from Customer Success expert Ed Powers that the brain is essentially an association machine. "It's easier for the brain to connect an image (or framework) with an abstract concept than it is to describe it using language and text."[72] The reason is symbols are much faster and easier to process by our intuitive subconscious than our effortful conscious brains. Visuals are so effective, because about 80 percent of our sensory computing power is visual processing. A study conducted on active learning showed that 10 to 20 percent of the participants were able to remember spoken and written information, while over 50 percent of visuals and images were remembered.[73] Words and text are stored in short-term memory, while images are stored in long-term memory.

...our brains process visual information more quickly and more easily than text.

The image in Figure 24[74] sums up the many letters, words, and paragraphs I use to communicate the importance of visuals. In fact, you probably will retain what is communicated in that image longer than the words you're reading now. Strategy expert Melissa Majors told me that our brains process every letter we see as a separate image. When you see images, you remember what you learned faster.[75] Since it's easier to process a visual signal more quickly than to read a sentence or a paragraph full of text, use graphics to share important information with your customers.

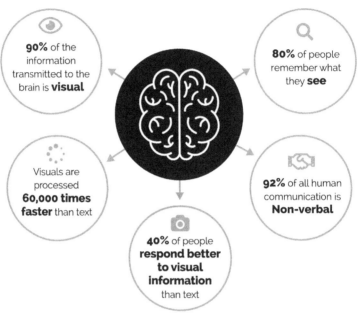

Figure 24: Humans Love Good Visuals

Take the time to create simple images

Save time when you communicate with customers by taking the time to create images. Start with representations that illustrate the onboarding journey you embark on together, then build on these as you progress throughout Orchestrated Onboarding. Include simple diagrams that illustrate the integrations and connections required to go live with your product. I often use the smart art features in most presentation applications. Once I have basic images, I rely on the expertise of graphic designers and

> *Save time when you communicate with customers by taking the time to create images.*

marketing teams to make the images look fabulous. Figure 25 shows examples using my Orchestrated Onboarding framework.

Start simple

EMBARK HANDOFF KICKOFF ADOPT REVIEW EXPAND

Convey what happens at each stage

EMBARK HANDOFF KICKOFF ADOPT REVIEW EXPAND

	EMBARK	HANDOFF	KICKOFF	ADOPT	REVIEW	EXPAND
PURPOSE	Partner for success Start strategic relationship	Align customer teams	Set up successful implementation	Implement Go live User training	Check in Drive to value	Customer maturity & expansion Maximize value
CUSTOMER	Onboarding overview	Overview for project team	Attend Kickoff	Complete tasks on time Attend training	Stakeholder attend Review	Drive user adoption
COMPANY	Attend handoff meeting	Hold alignment meeting	Provide project plan	Lead successful implementation	Share data	Proactive engagement
SUCCESS	Success plan reviewed	Sucess plan signed off	Kickoff meeting delivered	Successful go live	Process feedback	Achieve success plan & ongoing goals

Create a branded image

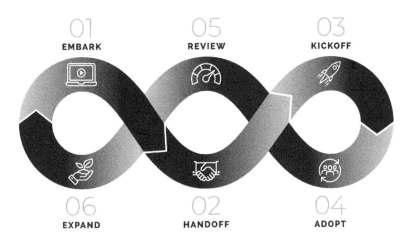

Figure 25: The Orchestrated Onboarding Framework

Show the progress

Customers want to know where they are in the process. When you show them visually, it reduces uncertainty and stress and even improves their overall experience working with you.

I incorporate visual images to convey the stages of working with my clients, and I'm amazed at how much people appreciate even basic descriptions of our journey together. See Figure 26 below. Showing progress keeps new and existing customers engaged along the onboarding journey and beyond. Use images to communicate important information, such as milestones, deliverables, and important points along the journey, and to show how far you have come. Visual images put the brain at ease and keeps people more engaged. It's like the tug at the end of a race. Even though you're tired, when you see the finish line you suddenly get a burst of energy to drive yourself forward. It's the same for customers when you show them how close they are to going live and achieving other milestones. This phenomenon is called the "goal gradient effect."[76]

Show progress along the journey

Figure 26: Progress Along the Onboarding Journey

Rather than playing tug-of-war with new customers, draw from neuroscience to align with the way brains process information. Move away from the overwhelm of too much text and toward images that convey important information during onboarding and implementation. Your customers will appreciate you for it.

Align Orchestrated Onboarding to your brand and processes

When I consult with companies, we start by mapping out the optimized onboarding approach with the six stages of Orchestrated Onboarding you now know: Embark, Handoff, Kickoff, Adopt, Review, and Expand. We map out the purpose and goals for each stage of onboarding. I use mind mapping software, XMind, to quickly capture these details as well as the roles, responsibilities, trigger, timing, collateral, meetings, and success metrics of each stage. After we detail the new approach, we tailor the framework to their brand and their internal processes. The name of each stage and the processes included need to make sense for both internal teams and customers. Here are examples of how several companies transformed their customer onboarding.

- **Workflow automation software:** Discover, Enable, Execute, Engage

- **Compliance software:** Discover, Collaborate, Connect, Comply, Optimize

- **Services company:** Launchpad, Ignition, Liftoff, and Voyage—to align with their rocket brand

- **Medical practice software:** Construct, Collaborate, Commence, Connect, Cultivate

- **Rebate management software:** Connect, Engage, Kick Off, Activate, Evolve

- **Analytics software:** Kickoff, Implement, Monitor, and Evolve

Once you have something that's workable, put the details into a comprehensive view in a slide to share with all the players in the "orchestra." Since Orchestrated Onboarding is by design a cross-functional approach, it's prudent to get buy-in from each team. If your onboarding journey starts before the deal closes, you'd better make sure the head of Sales is in alignment and willing to reinforce the new approach and all it entails.

After getting buy-in and updating the framework with feedback from other teams, reach out to Marketing teams and graphics designers to brand the onboarding framework and make it visually appealing and inspiring for both internal teams and customers. Then, take this attractive collateral and start introducing onboarding to prospects during the sales cycle. Put to use the high-level visual of how your company helps them at each stage of onboarding, and beyond.

Since Orchestrated Onboarding is by design a cross-functional approach, it's prudent to get buy-in from each team.

To see examples of customer-facing collateral and internal facing assets, go to OrchestratedOnboarding.com.

Start with high touch and then move to low and tech touch

When rolling out Orchestrated Onboarding for the first time, it usually makes sense to map out the new framework as a high touch approach. Start the process with dedicated resources to guide customers along each milestone and guidepost, possibly with an enterprise segment of customers. Assigning people to the onboarding tasks is a more flexible way to keep improving onboarding at your company. When things are rolling along smoothly, consider moving to a lower touch approach. Companies that have a mid-market customer segment may assign a pool of resources, rather than a dedicated CSM or onboarding specialist. The next stage is to explore a completely tech-touch approach with onboarding, enablement, and engagement content delivered through emails, inside your product interface, and in learning management systems. Chapter Thirteen covered ways to have a higher impact with less touch.

Initiating Orchestrated Onboarding at your company

Just because you have a new tailored framework and great visuals, doesn't mean your company will embrace the transformation. A successful rollout of any innovation, including Orchestrated Onboarding, includes these nine phases: communicate, execute, enable, pilot, operationalize, reinforce, market, measure, and maintain. Each phase uses best practices you learned in developing Orchestrated Onboarding, such as communications, measurements, and design thinking.

Communicate

Communication is important at all levels in your company. To unveil the new onboarding approach, it's helpful for everyone to know what's changing and why, as well as what's expected from them. Start with a company-wide announcement, but don't stop there. Many companies think that one big announcement is all they need to create change. However, research shows that redundancy is the solution to retention. It may take three, ten, or twenty times for people to hear the same thing before they change, so bake the repetition into your communication plan.

Start by assigning a communication plan owner. They can ensure the new program is communicated clearly and consistently across the company. Once you hold the company-wide meeting, then schedule team announcements, and work with managers to reinforce the changes with individual team members. Managers will be responsible for answering their questions and addressing their concerns.

Execute

The rollout includes creating and posting assets to make the new onboarding program a reality. Define and build the collateral for each onboarding stage. Next, create customer-facing and internal facing content, to indicate timing, roles, and responsibilities. I also have my clients create a central repository for all teams to access the current content and assign one person to maintain the site. Many of my clients create an internal site with a sub-site for each onboarding stage, including the main points, meeting agendas, and links to templates.

Enable

Deliver enablement to each team involved in Orchestrated Onboarding so they know how to work in harmony for a finely tuned customer experience. Since onboarding begins during the sales cycle, take care to include onboarding content in every sales enablement training. In addition, train Customer Success, Consulting, Support, and Training teams to ensure they are on board as well. Each person needs to comprehend their roles and responsibilities along every stage of the process. Show them where to find the assets and how to maximize them. Teach them how to provide feedback to improve the program. Schedule the training dates, deliver the training, and then follow up as needed.

Pilot

When you roll out new programs to customers, it's informative to pick a small group for the pilot. You might start with a specific segment of customers or with the customers of specific sales reps. As you launch Orchestrated Onboarding, consider working with a hand-picked team of sales reps, CSMs, and consultants to test drive the new framework, provide suggestions for improvement, and then update the program before you roll it out to your teams and to all your customers. Continue to monitor the new program closely—build in extra checkpoints and feedback sessions over the first several months to ensure the program is providing the expected impact.

Operationalize

A supply chain management company with whom I worked attempted to repeatedly fix their onboarding approach. Their hindrance was that onboarding never became a living process—it stayed static in slides and sheets filed away where they were rarely accessed. After we worked together to optimize their customer onboarding, I guided them to implement tools and systems to operationalize the program effectively. Take advantage of products specific for onboarding and/ or tailoring existing tools, such as CRMs and Customer Success platforms. That way you have a place to track where each new account is on their onboarding journey. In these systems, assign tasks to teams and customers. Keep people accountable. Provide management with dashboards and data to make insightful decisions.

Reinforce

Rolling out a new approach doesn't guarantee people in your company will change how they work. As a result, consider a reinforcement plan. Start by clearly defining what's expected of team members and gain agreement on what and how they need to change. Then, determine incentives and consequences to drive the new behavior. Consulting expert Alan Weiss shared with me that leveraging influencers and exemplars to guide teams is much more effective than carrots and sticks. "If you want to create change in an organization you have to change the exemplar person and you have to show them why it's in their best interest to change."[77] So, consider who's really on board with the new program. Who influences internal teams? Once you get them aligned with the new approach, others will quickly follow.

Market

Highlight your new onboarding program with prospects and customers. Many companies include overviews on their websites, and provide datasheets and testimonials to help people understand the value they provide beyond the initial sale. Review the go-to-market section in Chapter Fourteen to market your new offering effectively. Consider putting out a press release once you officially launch the new onboarding program.

Measure

How will you measure the success of your new onboarding program? Include relevant leading and lagging indicators, as discussed in Chapter Twelve. Capture a baseline and then measure trends quarterly. Metrics likely include the time it takes to onboard and implement new customers, product usage, and customer health scores. If you pilot with a specific segment of customers, you can compare one cohort to the other to see the impact Orchestrated Onboarding has on new accounts. Over time, you could possibly also contrast performance indicators of accounts before you rolled out the program and after.

Maintain

Review the principles of design thinking from Chapter Ten, and continue to update and iterate the onboarding process. Keep the program alive to keep maximizing value for customers. Learn what they want and need to keep refining. As your company grows, fine tune your program to scale, to be more efficient, and to have more impact. You'll probably start with high-touch programs, and then tailor low- and tech-touch approaches for appropriate segments. As you update the program assets and collateral, ensure all team members have easy access to the latest versions. Continue to communicate clearly, deliver training, and hold feedback sessions, to keep Orchestrated Onboarding alive and well at your company. It helps to have one owner of the program to maintain the content and to communicate it out to the relevant teams.

WHAT MATTERS

» Include visuals to improve communication with new customers as images are quicker to process and easier to remember.

» Tailor the six stages and collateral of the Orchestrated Onboarding framework to align with your processes and branding.

» Incorporate all nine phases of rolling out the Orchestrated Onboarding framework to have the most success at your organization: communicate, execute, enable, pilot, operationalize, reinforce, market, measure, and maintain.

READY TO ONBOARD?

» Who can help you to turn your collateral into visually appealing and easy to process images?

» What is a good pilot group to start Orchestrated Onboarding with?

» Who is a good person on your team to update and maintain the collateral and assets of your onboarding program?

CHAPTER **16**

Conclusion

As you now realize, the work of implementing Orchestrated Onboarding is not trivial. It requires collaboration across silos in your own business, and moving closer to understanding your customers' needs. But everyone benefits. Your new customers realize the real value of the solutions you sell. Your business gains more loyal, long-standing customers and the revenues they contribute. And if you work in Customer Success, you become a proactive partner in everyone's success, rather than a heroic problem-solver always under stress. The Orchestrated Onboarding framework brings the whole orchestra in tune.

As you can tell by now, I truly believe we make companies successful by engaging their customers and the people using the products without hesitation. This requires building trusting relationships, breaking down silos, exploring ways to scale, and providing prescriptive,

> *...we make companies successful by engaging their customers and the people using the products without hesitation.*

proactive, and frictionless experiences for customers. That's why it's a sophisticated seamless customer journey, beginning with onboarding.

Start orchestrating

When you leverage the six stages of Orchestrated Onboarding with new customers, you Embark on a new journey together and partner for success, even before a customer signs a contract. To align internal and customer teams, you hold internal and customer Handoffs. That allows you to Kickoff implementation projects more successfully and guide users to Adopt your product. Then strategically Review how the new account is doing to keep them successful and Expand their value in your product.

I urge you to use the Orchestrated Onboarding framework with a handful of customers immediately. See what you can do to make a difference. Then, execute the framework across a whole segment of customers, including different customer types, which might be consumers as well as businesses. Even your partners benefit from an Orchestrated Onboarding framework. Pick one area to start today, and please let me know how it's going. I'd love to connect.

Go to my website

I invite you to my website to leverage resources, share stories, and connect: **www.donnaweber.com**

Glossary

This glossary provides an overview of Customer Success and financial terms.

Customer Success Terms

Buyer journey: The buyer journey is the sum of experiences that buyers go through when interacting with your company. Buyers interact with sales teams as they move from being leads to prospects through your sales funnel.

Churn: A regular, quantifiable process or rate of change that occurs in a business over a period of time as existing customers are lost and new customers are added.

Cost of customer retention (CORE): The cost to retain existing customers.

Cross-sell: To sell a different product or service to existing customers.

Customer acquisition costs (CAC): The cost associated in convincing a customer to buy a product/service.

Customer journey: The sum of experiences that customers go through after they sign a contract with your company, the customer journey happens after the buyer journey. During this time, customers interact with post-sales teams such as Customer Success, Consulting, and Support.

Customer health score: Includes a number of criteria which are leading indicators to accurately assess the current state of accounts.

Customer onboarding: The action or process of familiarizing new customers with your products and services; customer onboarding is the first part of the customer journey. It includes these important elements: building customer relationships, implementation and going live with your product, user adoption, and change management.

Gross retention revenue (GRR): Amount of dollars retained from a previously defined cohort of customers/contracts.

First value: The moment when customers first realize the value of your product.

High touch: Providing a very close relationship with customers, generally at a one-to-one level when assisting them with implementations and solving customer problems.

Lagging indicators: Usually includes renewal rates, net retention, and total lifetime value, which may take several months or years to calculate.

Land and expand: The process where a company lands an initial small deal within a customer, then continues to sell additional projects and uses into different organizations with that customer.

Leading indicators: Metrics along the customer journey such as product usage, customer satisfaction, and services received, which are used to predict performance.

Lifetime value (LTV): A prediction of the net profit attributed to the entire future relationship with a customer.

Low touch: Providing one-to-many relationships with customers where services are delivered at scale.

Net retention revenue (NRR): The percentage of recurring revenue retained from existing customers in a defined time period, including expansion revenue, downgrades, and cancellations. Companies with greater net retention grow faster.

Recurring revenue: Revenue which compounds month-over-month, or year-over-year, leading to huge profits when customers keep renewing. Companies may use metrics based on either monthly recurring revenue (MRR) or annual recurring revenue (ARR).

Renewal: Granting or obtaining an extension of the subscription.

Subscription: An arrangement for providing, receiving, or making use of a product or service on a continuing or periodic basis. This is often implemented with a prepayment plan for an initial term.

Tech touch: Automating services with customers so individuals at your company are not directly involved with customer interactions.

Upsell: When a customer purchases a larger consumption contract than the previous contract. Upsells drive NRR.

Valuable Financial Terms

Attach rate: A measure of how many add-on products your business sells with each license deal. For example, when it comes to selling premium packages, attach rate measures the percentage of deals sold that include the services offering. The higher the attach rate, the better for enabling customers.

Bookings: The amount of money customers commit to spending with your company. Bookings are tracked when a deal closes or a contract is signed. However, the money is likely not collected or recognized by accounting at that point in time.

Cost center: A cost center is a department within a company that does not directly add to the company's profit. While cost centers contribute indirectly to a company's profitability, they add operating costs to the business bottom line. Margins are negative in a cost center.

Cost recovery center: Also known as a "break-even" center, this is a department within a company that has the goal of having a zero profit. Rather than being a cost to a company, the goal is to invest all profits back into the department, to keep the organization growing.

Margin: Refers to the difference between the cost to create a product and the selling price. Margins appear as percentages of net sales revenues. A positive margin means you're making a profit. A negative margin means you're incurring costs. A zero margin means you're breaking even.

Profit and loss center: A profit and loss center (P&L) is a department within a company that contributes to profitability directly through its actions. It's treated virtually as a separate, standalone business, responsible for generating revenues and earnings. Profit and losses are calculated separately on accounting balance sheets, with the goal to have positive margins.

Revenue: The money actually received for products.

Revenue recognition: The time when revenue is officially recognized, usually when the product is delivered or the service is actually provided. In subscription offerings, revenue is often ratable, which means the accounting team recognizes revenue for a one-year license over 12 months, at 1/12th the total amount each month.

References

[1] The 2020 Customer Onboarding Report, Springboard Solutions https://mailchi. mp/b2fc9e1caa2c/onboarding-report

[2] Tara-Nicholle Nelson, "Helping Customers Along Their Journey," ServiceRocket, Podcast audio, March 13, 2017. http://blog.servicerocket.com/podcasts/ep.-34- tara-nicholle-nelson-on-helping-customers-along-their-journey

[3] Alex, "The Three Leading Causes of Customer Churn," November 20, 2015. https://www.retently.com/blog/three-leading-causes-churn/

[4] CallMiner, "The CallMiner Churn Index 2020," n.d. https://learning.callminer. com/c/whitepaper-churn-index-utilities?x=CFl8z6&lx=amFxJO&search=index

[5] 60 Experiments: What Vista Equity Partners Learned From Deploying Customer Success Across the Portfolio," Gainsight Pulse recap videos, May 2019. https://www. gainsight.com/pulse/2019/recap/

[6] Conversation with Ed Powers, 2020.

[7] Ed Powers, "Why a CSM's First Impression Means So Much," Service Excellence Partners, May 19, 2014. https://se-partners.com/why-a-csms-first-impression- means-so-much/

[8] Brian Anderson, "First Impressions and Onboarding: Shaping Expectations," BambooHR, March 30, 2017. https://www.bamboohr.com/blog/first-impressions- onboarding/

[9] Shahram Heshmat, "What Is Confirmation Bias?" Psychology Today. Sussex Publishers, April 23, 2015. https://www.psychologytoday.com/us/blog/science- choice/201504/what-is-confirmation-bias

[10] Ibid.

[11] Zachary Crockett, "How to Avoid Buyer's Remorse," The Hustle, February 23, 2019. https://thehustle.co/how-to-avoid-buyers-remorse/

[12] A.W. Kruglanski & S. Fishman, (2009). The need for cognitive closure. In M. R. Leary & R. H. Hoyle (Eds.), Handbook of individual differences in social behavior (p. 343– 3). The Guilford Press. https://psycnet.apa.org/record/2009-12071-023

[13] Conversation with Ed Powers, 2020.

[14]Greg Daines, "The Cardinal Sin of Client Success," May 21, 2020 https://www.clientsuccess.com/resources/webinars/customer-success-webinar-series-the-cardinal-sin-of-client-success/

[15]Customer Acquisition Cost. Klipfolio MeticHQ https://www.klipfolio.com/metrics/finance/customer-acquisition-cost

[16]Neil Patel, "Customer Acquisition Cost: The One Metric That Can Determine Your Company's Fate," January 24, 2020. https://neilpatel.com/blog/customer-acquisition-cost/

[17]Charles Atkins, Shobhit Gupta, and Paul Roche, "Introducing Customer Success 2.0: The New Growth Engine," February 20, 2019. https://www.mckinsey.com/industries/high-tech/our-insights/introducing-customer-success-2-0-the-new-growth-engine

[18]Ben Murray, "Committed Monthly Recurring Revenue (CMRR) Defined," May 11, 2017 https://www.thesaascfo.com/committed-monthly-recurring-revenue/

[19]Fred Reichheld, "Prescription for Cutting Costs," n.d. https://media.bain.com/Images/BB_Prescription_cutting_costs.pdf

[20]Nicolas Maechler, Kevin Neher, and Robert Park, "From Touchpoints to Journeys: Seeing the World as Customers Do," McKinsey & Company, June 4, 2019 https://www.mckinsey.com/business-functions/marketing-and-sales/our-insights/from-touchpoints-to-journeys-seeing-the-world-as-customers-do

[21]Joey Coleman, Never Lose a Customer Again, p. 61 (Portfolio/Penguin, 2018).

[22]How To Create a Customer Success Plan: A Step-by-Step Guide to Delivering on Expectation and Ensuring Success. ServiceSource, n.d. https://www.servicesource.com/wp-content/uploads/2018/04/white-paper-how-to-create-a-customer-success-plan.pdf

[23]Joey Coleman, Never Lose a Customer Again, p. 25, (Portfolio/Penguin, 2018).

[24]Lincoln Murphy, "Nail the Handoffs," Gainsight, August 15, 2019. http://www.gainsight.com/customer-success-best-practices/nail-the-handoffs

[25]Natalie Macks, "The Critical Sales-Success Handoff," The Success League, July 15, 2015. http://www.thesuccessleague.io/blog/2015/7/15/the-critical-sales-success-handoff

[26]Joey Coleman, Never Lose a Customer Again, p. 146 (Portfolio/Penguin, 2018).

[27]"What is Change Management?" n. d.https://www.prosci.com/resources/articles/what-is-change-management

[28]"Change Management" n.d. https://organizationalexcellence.virginia.edu/change-management

[29]The Success League, "Quarterly Business Reviews" course https://www.thesuccessleague.io/csm-training-program/quarterly-business-reviews

[30]Michael Booz, "These 3 Industries Have the Highest Talent Turnover Rates," March 15, 2018.https://business.linkedin.com/talent-solutions/blog/trends-and-research/2018/the-3-industries-with-the-highest-turnover-rates%0A

[31] Donna Weber, "The 80/20 Rule of Customer Education," January 15, 2018 https://www.springboardin.com/blog/the-80-20-rule-of-customer-education

[32] Conversations with Mike Gospe, 2018.

[33] Customers 2020: The Future of B-To-B Customer Experience. Walker, n.d. https://www.walkerinfo.com/Portals/0/Documents/Knowledge%20Center/Featured%20Reports/WALKER-Customers2020.pdf

[34] Rikke Friis Dam and Teo Yu Siang, "5 Stages in the Design Thinking Process," The Interaction Design Foundation, July 23, 2020. http://www.interaction-design.org/literature/article/5-stages-in-the-design-thinking-process

[35] Sarah Gibbons, "Design Thinking 101," Nielsen Norman Group, July 31, 2016. https://www.nngroup.com/articles/design-thinking/

[36] Rikke Friis Dam and Teo Yu Siang, "Design Thinking: Getting Started with Empathy," The Interaction Design Foundation, August 13, 2018. https://www.interaction-design.org/literature/article/design-thinking-getting-started-with-empathy

[37] Conversations with Mike Gospe, 2018.

[38] Conversation with Mikael Blaisdell, 2018.

[39] Eric Almquist, Jamie Cleghorn, and Lori Sherer, "What B2B Buyers Really Care About," Harvard Business Review, Mar-Apr 2018 http://hbr.org/2018/03/the-b2b-elements-of-value

[40] Conversations with Mike Gospe, 2018.

[41] Eric Almquist, Jamie Cleghorn, and Lori Sherer, "What B2B Buyers Really Care About," Harvard Business Review, Mar-Apr 2018 http://hbr.org/2018/03/the-b2b-elements-of-value

[42] Customers 2020: The Future of B-To-B Customer Experience. Walker, n.d. https://www.walkerinfo.com/Portals/0/Documents/Knowledge%20Center/Featured%20Reports/WALKER-Customers2020.pdf

[43] Ibid.

[44] "Gartner Hype Cycle," Gartner, n.d. https://www.gartner.com/en/research/methodologies/gartner-hype-cycle

[45] Ibid.

[46] "Time to Value (TTV)," Baremetrics, October 25, 2017. https://baremetrics.com/academy/time-to-value-ttv

[47] Shreesha Ramdas, "Should CS Care about Fastest Time-to-Value?," Strikedeck, May 28, 2019.https://strikedeck.com/should-cs-care-about-fastest-time-to-value/

[48] Conversation with Brian Gentile, 2020.

[49] Patrick Campbell, "Subscription Revenue Model: How Subscriptions Makes Money & Why Subscription-Based Revenue Works," Profitwell, September 12, 2020. https://www.profitwell.com/blog/subscription-revenue-model

[50]"Mastering the Art of the Outcome: How Guru Turned Customer Success Into a Company Cornerstone," First Round Review, July 16, 2019. https://firstround.com/review/mastering-the-art-of-the-outcome-how-guru-turned-customer-success-into-a-company-cornerstone/

[51]"Time to Value (TTV)," Baremetrics, October 25, 2017. https://baremetrics.com/academy/time-to-value-ttv

[52]Ramdas, "Should CS Care," 2019.

[53]ServiceSource, "Creating Customers for Life," 2017. https://jp.servicesource.com/wp-content/uploads/2018/04/ebook-creating-customers-for-life-rlm.pdf

[54]Mikael Blaisdell presentation at Customer SuccessCon, Berkeley, California, 2019.

[55]Nello Franco, "Time to First Value: A Key Metric," August 25, 2015. https://blog.nellofranco.com/tag/enablement/

[56]"Time to Value (TTV)," Baremetrics, October 25, 2017. https://baremetrics.com/academy/time-to-value-ttv

[57]Donna Weber, "Customer Success and Value Provability," Customer Success Association, August 18, 2019. https://www.customersuccessassociation.com/customer-success-and-value-provability/.

[58] Lincoln Murphy, Customer Success Meetup, February 23, 2018.

[59]Bill Cushard, "5 Factors That Limit Start-up Growth by Zack Urlocker," Company Blog, March 14, 2014. http://blog.servicerocket.com/adoption/blog/2014/03/start-up-growth.

[60]Lauren Thibodeau, "It's A Jungle Out There - Of Content That Is (Part 1)," CEdMA, June 4, 2019. https://www.cedma.org/blog/its-a-jungle-out-there-of-content-that-is-part-1

[61]Daniela Di Noi, "Do Workers Still Waste Time Searching for Information?," Xenit, May 22, 2018. https://blog.xenit.eu/blog/do-workers-still-waste-time-searching-for-information

[62]Thibodeau, "It's a Jungle Out There," 2019.

[63]Donna Weber, "It's A Jungle Out There - Of Content That Is (Part 2)," CEdMA, June 18, 2019. https://www.cedma.org/blog/its-a-jungle-out-there-of-content-that-is-part-2

[64]Adam Avramescu, "Customers Don't Care about Using Your Product (so Don't Educate Them like They Do)," LinkedIn, March 22, 2017. https://www.linkedin.com/pulse/customers-dont-care-using-your-product-so-educate-them-adam-avramescu/

[65]Gainsight, "Charging for Customer Success," SlideShare, January 12, 2016. https://www.slideshare.net/GainsightHQ/charging-for-customer-success-56974347

[66]David Clarke and Ron Kinghorn, "Experience Is Everything: Here's How to Get It Right." PWC, 2018. https://www.pwc.com/us/en/advisory-services/publications/consumer-intelligence-series/pwc-consumer-intelligence-series-customer-experience.pdf

[67]"Build and Launch Service Offers That Drive Value for Customers, Technology Services Industry Association," 2019. https://www.tsia.com/conference-presentations/build-and-launch-service-offers-that-drive-value-for-customers

[68]"Go to Market," Wikipedia, August 11, 2020. http://en.wikipedia.org/wiki/Go_to_market

[69]Echo Rivera, "6 Reasons You Need Good Visuals in Your Presentations," Updated January 2020. https://www.echorivera.com/blog/6reasonsvisuals

[70]"Why Are Visuals Important in Marketing?" n.d. https://www.brightedge.com/glossary/importance-of-visuals-in-marketing

[71]Rachel Gillett, "We We're More Likely to Remember Content with Images and Video," September 18, 2014. https://www.fastcompany.com/3035856/why-were-more-likely-to-remember-content-with-images-and-video-infogr

[72]Conversation with Ed Powers, 2020.

[73]Echo Brown, "Why Visual Communication Is Important," August 10, 2017 https://www.eztalks.com/unified-communications/why-visual-communicaion-is-important.html

[74]Tony Seel, "How to Up Your Game with Visual Content Marketing," May 7, 2019. https://www.tonyseel.com/how-to-up-your-game-visual-content-marketing/

[75]Melissa Majors, "How to Design and Deliver Brain-Friendly Presentations," n.d. https://learn.melissamajors.com/courses/Brain-Friendly

[76]"Goal Gradient Effect," n.d. https://www.coglode.com/research/goal-gradient-effect

[77]Conversation with Alan Weiss, 2020.

Acknowledgements

First of all, I'd like to acknowledge all the companies I work with and for. It is a privilege and a pleasure every day to learn and work together as we guide customers to value.

It's an honor to be part of the Customer Success, Customer Education, and Customer Experience communities where there's a generosity of spirit, connection, and support.

For encouraging me to write, I'd like to thank Mike Gospe. Mike suggested I start a daily writing process several years ago when we first met over coffee in Los Altos, CA. Tara Mohr's encouragement during her Playing Big course got me to put my writing out there, regardless of who reads it. Janet Gregory and Karyn Holl provided continued support and guidance along the way.

For reading the book in development and providing valuable feedback I'd like to acknowledge Samma Hafeez and Elizabeth Jones.

I would also like to recognize Samma Hafeez for generously writing the book foreword. It's a privilege to be on the journey together.

I am grateful for Anne Janzer's gentle and invaluable guidance to improve my writing and to "get the word out." Thank you for helping me to enjoy the journey.

Linda Popky was instrumental in providing the book title and valuable editing.

I truly appreciate Carla Green for doing an amazing job on the book layout.

Roderick Jefferson helped me see how too often Customer Success teams use "hope as a strategy."

Brian Gentile continues to be an inspiration for my work and models great leadership. Thank you for championing the work I do and for sending high growth companies my way.

I am indebted to Ed Powers for turning me on to the fascinating world of neuroscience and the impact it has on customer onboarding. There's so much more to learn!

Alan Weiss is instrumental in keeping me focused on being The Customer Onboarding Expert and providing value to my clients.

Juli Johns is key to turning my concepts to visuals. Thank you for creating the Orchestrated Onboarding and Customer Success Bow Tie images, as well as all the images in *Onboarding Matters*.

Leona DeVinne injects joy into my work and keeps me on track in my business and life in general.

I appreciate Linda Galindo and Francoise Tourniaire for encouraging me to focus on what I know.

Becky Heaman is essential in keeping things going behind the scenes.

And of course, I am forever grateful to my husband, Ed Roseboom, who reads all my articles, listens to my ideas and challenges, and is an ongoing foundation of love, acceptance, and adventure.

About the Author

Donna Weber is the world's leading expert in customer onboarding. For more than two decades, she's helped high-growth startups and established enterprises create customers for life.

Donna is a recognized Customer Success thought leader, influencer, strategist, advisor, author, and speaker who gets to the heart of the matter. She is passionate about helping customers reach their goals, because when customers win, you win. It's that simple.

High growth companies hire Donna to increase customer retention, decrease time to customer first value, increase customer lifetime value, reduce implementation time and costs, increase product usage and adoption, and scale Customer Success organizations.

Prior to founding her boutique consulting firm in 2016, Donna worked at several startups, where she built Customer Success and Customer Education programs and organizations from scratch.

When she's not orchestrating customer onboarding, you will find her outside, hiking or cycling the hills of the San Francisco Bay Area, or kayaking the waters of California and beyond.

Donna lives in Palo Alto, California, with her husband, Ed. Donna is a graduate of the University of California at San Diego.

To learn more about Donna's work, visit **donnaweber.com**.

49297851R00122